Your

College Student

Needs

Your Prayers

Monica Renahan

Incremental Good Productions

Copies of this book can be purchased in bulk for group fundraising or educational use. Learn about the program details online at: **www.lifeasacollegemom101.wordpress.com**.

The internet addresses referenced here and throughout this book are valid as of the print date. All reasonable attempts will be made to link any updated addresses to those printed.

The bible verses quoted are scripture taken from the HOLY BIBLE, NEW INTERNATIONAL VERSION ®. Copyright ©1973, 1978, 1984 by International Bible Society. Used by permission of Zondervan Publishing House. All rights reserved.

ISBN 978-1-7374684-5-5

Cover Photo by Canva Design

Table of Contents

A note to start…

Let's start with my Author's Disclaimer: I'm a college mom. I lived through lots of things sending two kids to college, and I witnessed the process as many of my friends and family members lived through it over the past 15 years. I'm not a psychologist, relationship guru, spiritual teacher, or Biblical scholar. This isn't a how-to guide or a deep spiritual study on blessing your child's college experience. It just helps you pray about what matters.

I wrote these chapters based on stories that other college moms told me. I pulled together the advice and experiences of many women who offered to share the things that mattered in their college student's life after Moving In Day. Seeing all the challenges that our students face, I picked out areas for prayer which might not be as obvious as they seem. Most of the 50 topics apply to college life throughout all four years, but some focus specifically on newcomers to college campuses. You may start reading a new chapter and find it does not apply in your student's life right now. You can skip it, but remember to go back to it if something comes up. I'm sure you will find plenty of things that make you think and help you connect more with your daughter or son. (Throughout this book, you can switch the words "daughter" and "son" at any time to make the things you read apply to your own circumstances. I use a mix of both to make the chapters relevant to anyone.) I wrote specifically for other moms, but dads or other family members can read along, too.

Since every student's college challenges are different, even experienced moms can find new things to pray about almost every day. Join me and hundreds of other moms across the country as we build a routine of praying for our college kids!

Time to share my Thank You List:

To my husband, Jim – You inspire me and you fill my heart.

To my daughters, Sarah and Marie – You each bring me joy.

To my editor, Amy Scharf – You are amazing in all you do.

To my good friend Jill Epperson – You listen to me and encourage me.

To my mom, Monica Novak – You were my example.

To all my friends who helped me learn about parenting over the past six years (or longer), especially by praying, sharing parenting stories, advising, taking surveys, being a friend, or reading the early versions of this book:

Mary Allen	Deidra Gennaro	Kristie Davis-Noles
Deanna Altomara	Jennifer Hayden	Linda Perry
Andrée Beaver	Tony Head	Jennifer Potter
Lisa Boyle	Annie Hocter	Patti Redman
Joann Centrone	Jennifer Hollinger	Andrea Rietman
Brian Comstock	Cheryl Kight	Carmen Ruckman
Kristine Cordts	Jill Klein	Laura Sharrett
Joyce Davis	Jody Koch	Evi Slaby
Cheryle Delzoppo	Serena Laroia	Brooksie Smith
Gretchen Easterday	Sylvia Labitzke	Gracie Sung
Lucinda Rinehart Embry	Stephen Maginas	Jahara Tapal
JJ Epperson	Beth Marmion	Lisa Trockman
Flourish Writers Community	Heather Maroo	Susan Turner
Liesl Fraley	Angie Menke	Chip Wamsley
Jennifer Gallant	Kay Morris	Melissa Werner

...And plenty of other good friends and good moms who shared a bit of their lives for these pages and on my blog **Life As A College Mom 101**. Find it at www.lifeasacollegemom101.wordpress.com .

1 Moving from the Big Picture to the Things That Matter Today

Ask twenty moms, "What things would you pray about for your college student?" and you would get some of these answers:

Good Grades	Safety
Choosing a Major	New Responsibilities
Choosing a Career	Health and Avoiding Illness
Getting Through Difficult Classes	Getting Sleep
Friends & Roommates	Meeting Deadlines
Tests, Exams, and Finals	… and for A Good Year

They're all good answers. They definitely cover the top ten. There's something missing, though. What these answers leave out is a little more insightful than any of their topics: not one answer mentions any details. Most prayers from college moms cover things with a blanket approach. These prayers include their concerns but avoid any specifics. The big, wide, groundcover prayer works for them: "Hit all the big topics with a huge prayer blanket and they'll be okay," sums it up. As the weeks go by, most college moms start modifying their general prayers. They get more personal by adding the names of new friends, or maybe the specific illness they want their son to avoid since his floor has become a breeding ground for it. Maybe a mom prays that a daughter finally understands the concepts in a particular class. Every one of those prayers for little details has relevance and value. "Mom Prayers" matter. They have sustained our children for years.

As their needs have changed, the prayers we've prayed have changed. When our kids were little, they came to us with their fears and failures. They asked for help and looked for our compassion. They needed guidance once their emotions subsided. We prayed for their minds and hearts and experiences. We prayed for them to grow.

Now, as emerging adults, they have stepped into a new life as college students. They have cut the cord in some areas, but they will hold on firmly in others as they make their way in a new place. Surrounded by new experiences and people, they will create their own lives. We need to change the focus of our prayers to the things that matter to them now. Finding out which things matter and what to focus on will challenge you.

Sometimes college students change to a minimal level of communication with their parents when they move away. They stop sharing as many details of their lives. They shift from spending many hours each day in our presence to living an independent life. You can try to get the details out of your son or encourage your daughter to update you on how she keeps busy, but the dynamic has changed. They might share some relevant details if you ask the right question. They may call you for important things. But the little experiences that touch their lives will remain untold stories on their internal hard drives, unless you happen to catch a mention of them on Twitter.

A friend told me this story:

> I saw an old friend across the checkout lines at the grocery store. She didn't look good. She had her head down and her body language screamed, "I'm furious right now." Twice I saw her reach for her phone, look at a text, and tighten up even more. When she started emptying her cart, she accidentally dropped her phone, and it slid across the floor toward me. We both stooped down to pick it up, and when we made eye contact, I could tell she was on the verge of tears. When she recognized me, all I could say was, "Hi, how's it going?"

She looked down again and said, "This mothering stuff… some days…," and then she turned to move up in her aisle. With magazines and candy blocking me from continuing, I could have left it at that. It was a perfect opportunity for me to drop it and walk away. Something told me not to. I looked over the racks of gum and mints, and I saw a lady who might need a friend. She might not, too, and that could be awkward. But I finished checking out at the same time she did, and we headed toward the door.

"How is your son doing at college?" I said, just wanting to reopen the conversation.

"I have no idea. He hasn't called in almost three weeks. His dad and I wanted to stop and see him when we were driving through there this weekend and we still haven't heard back except for a text that said, 'Isn't there a game on Saturday?' What's that supposed to mean? He's busy and won't carve a few hours out of his schedule to spend time with us? Maybe there's something else important going on, and that's fine, but how would I know? He never tells us anything about his life anymore."

I knew what she meant, but I had never admitted it to anyone. My oldest daughter had been like that. No responses to texts; phone calls went unanswered. We were lucky to get a three-sentence summary of the semester when she came home on break. Most of her life no longer involved us, so she didn't feel the need for small talk about things that happened at college. Her independence had taken root, and she was doing just fine on her own. It would have been nice to know about it, though.

I told my friend, "Sometimes our college kids forget that we've been a part of their lives for the past 18 years, and we'd like to have that continue. It's hard when they close us out. But, I'm telling you, I can always find something to pray about for my kids. That's the way I keep them in my mind. Even if I don't know the specific details about their lives, I can pray for lots of things. Sometimes I'll send them a text saying, 'I was praying for you today. I hope things are good.'"

She looked at me and said, "I wouldn't even know what to pray about. Grades, roommates… what else is there?"

That was the big picture. I knew in her heart there were plenty more things to cover. She just needed to think a little and get a few suggestions along the way. It was a start.

It's your time to start, too. You can remain a casual observer, hovering with your prayer blanket at 20,000 feet. You can hit the high points and low points and add a few significant details once in a while. Doing that seems to make a difference sometimes. If you keep that up, though, it will not help you stay connected to meaningful things that happen in your student's life.

Maybe it's time to try something new.

Every chapter of this book brings you out of the clouds and back down to earth on things that matter to college students and to their parents. Each topic combines stories of other moms' experiences with topical prayer ideas and some practical day-by-day things that can become your prayer requests. Not every topic applies to every student, and every mother has different prayer needs. But, until you read some of these chapters, you may not know what your child finds challenging about campus life. You may not hear about her struggles with responsibilities or decisions. Reading about someone else's needs may bring them to your awareness and help prepare you for the day when your son asks for advice about them, too. This book is full of suggestions on what you can pray about which probably will matter in your student's life sometime during their college years.

Walk through these chapters with an open mind. You may find new opportunities to start discussions with your son about schoolwork and other obligations. You may also build your prayer arsenal for some future moment when a new conflict arises. By praying for your daughter's upcoming challenges along with the things she currently faces, you're building your defense against the impending moments of chaos and conflict which will invade as she lives her life at college.

What can you do?

Sometimes when these challenges come our way, we don't have a specific solution for them. There's nothing we can do to help resolve the situation or clarify a response. When that happens, I encourage you to take some time to think about your college student's capabilities and remove yourself from the responsibility to fix things. Instead, it would be a great time to turn to God and ask for a little help in prayer. Plenty of parents like you and me spend a good deal of time praying for our sons and daughters as they grow up. Don't stop now!

Praying for our sons and daughters can strengthen them and us. It will give your concerns a voice as you go over the details of the situation you're facing. It will clear your thinking as you take time to reflect and prioritize your concerns. By asking for support beyond your own abilities, you sometimes uncover things you still can do to help in the situation.

Prayer and reflection help in many ways, but if you're not a praying person, I encourage you to use the suggested prayers as thinking points for ways to help your student in whatever he or she faces. If nothing else, use them to open up a dialogue for resolving a struggle and offering support along the way.

So, what can you do right now? Pray.

Prayers for Today

Pray that your prayers change from the wide ranging to the specific.

Pray that you take time daily to think about your son's needs and pray specifically for them.

Pray for an understanding of your daughter's new status as an independent college student.

Pray that the communication between you and your son stays vibrant.

Pray for open sharing of the important challenges your daughter faces.

Pray that your student will use you as a resource. Also pray that you learn to listen without advising and then offer to help sort things out without solving it all when they ask for your support.

What else will you pray for?

As you go through these topics, I'd love to hear how you pray for your college student. The stories you share and the lessons you have learned may make someone else's experience a little easier. Let's keep an open dialogue going. Feel free to include your prayers, stories, and comments on my website, "Life as a College Mom 101" — I look forward to reading your replies. **www.lifeasacollegemom101@wordpress.com**

> For a word of encouragement about your prayers, remember what the Bible says in Philippians 4:6-7 (NIV): "Do not be anxious in anything, but in everything, by prayer and petition, with thanksgiving, present your requests to God. And the peace of God, which transcends all understanding, will guard your hearts and minds in Christ Jesus."

2 Preparing Them for College

Whatever you did to get ready to send your student off to college, you probably made some mistakes along the way. Looking back, you may have some regrets. Maybe you wish you could have guided your daughter down an entirely different path (… if only you had been more persuasive). You may have encouraged your son to participate in a stepping stone activity to open future doors, and then watched his interests shift to something completely different. You tried things and then decided to try something else.

Your student probably agrees the route he took wasn't perfect. If you ask ten parents to describe the perfect path to prepare for college, you would get ten different answers. And, if you ask the same question to their ten students, you would get ten more options, all with unique perspectives. You would find some common ground along the way, but no one has designed the perfect, one-size-fits-all method. So give yourself a little grace. Accept that no matter how hard you tried, your child's preparation has not been complete.

Right now is a good time to consider another change in perspective: you cannot prepare for all that your daughter will deal with as she starts college. That's okay. That's what every mom throughout college history has faced. Each one has sent her kids off with great pride in the rock-solid preparation she gave them. Then she reacts with shock and disbelief the first time they stumble along the way.

Even if you use what you learned by sending your first kid away to college, your second kid won't have the perfect preparation to go off to school. Even if you have five kids, sending the first four will not prepare you for everything that the fifth will face. What #1 needs as a Pre-Med student and athlete will differ from #2's needs for programming computers and spending time on student government. Your social butterfly will encounter different challenges than your quiet observer. A planner will find that things don't always fit her rigid schedule, while a procrastinator will try to create time when there's none left before a deadline. What your well-prepared son knows now will not provide all he needs to make it through the next four years.

Don't feel bad. This scenario has a 100% mom-inclusion rate. Every single mom who has gone through this can tell you a story (or many, many stories) about the things she wishes her kid had been ready for before getting to college. No one has a comprehensive "Don't Leave Home Without Knowing This" list. No one has created the perfect checklist to complete before move-in day. You've done your best to raise a competent child and you've led him to the door. Now he needs to walk through it and start taking his own steps into adulthood.

What can you do?

Prayers for Today

Pray for the completeness of your preparations, that your daughter has absorbed what you taught her and has taken it to heart.

Pray that as new challenges come your son's way, he can combine the practical knowledge he has with his creativity and come up with a good solution to whatever he faces.

Pray that as your daughter struggles with new obstacles, she reaches out for support from others (and even from you) to give her the skills, knowledge, or direction she needs to succeed.

Pray for finding out things you've forgotten and filling the gaps before they cause difficulties.

What else will you pray for?

3 Germs, Germs, and More Germs

Every school joined the fight against the Covid virus, working to kill any contaminants before they multiply. You would think any other germs out there would also die from all the disinfecting, but it only takes a few microbe survivors to keep more sickness spreading.

Some college students make it through their first semester without catching a cold. Others become sickness attractors and have germs attaching to them like moths drawn to porch lights. Then they realize they are not as invincible as they thought. You may find yourself on the receiving end of a late-night phone call like this...

"Mom? (You hear a sniffle and a stifled cough.) I'm sick."

"How bad do you feel?" (Your Mom Radar clicks on to scan the situation).

"I don't know. Pretty awful. I can't breathe through my nose and my throat hurts more now because I have to breathe through my mouth," she says.

"Well, it's good that you're still managing to breathe. Keep that up." (Deflect with humor).

"But Mom, (cough, wheeze, sniffle, sniffle), I don't know what to do. I have a test and a group project tomorrow, but I don't know if I can even think right now (cough, cough, cough)," she says.

"Try to eat something. That will give you some energy. Maybe drink hot tea, too."

"I can't get anything now, Mom. All the cafeterias closed at 9pm. I don't have any tea either." (Your alert bells go off. No support services. This could get bad.)

"Then try to get some sleep. I'm sure you'll feel better if you rest," you offer. (You can tell she feels miserable.)

"Every time I put my head down, my sinuses start draining down my throat. If I'm choking, I can't sleep."

"Maybe you could prop up your head by folding your pillow in half to make it thicker, or use your puffy coat rolled up behind your pillow. Then just close your eyes. It will help."

Right about then, you start fighting your internal battle: you want to help but you need to stay in a support mode, not a control mode. You have at least five things to suggest, including waking up her roommate to get a ride to a nearby store to buy tissues (the soft ones), along with soup, decongestant, and disinfectant wipes. You want to call her RA, dorm director, professors, group project members, and the daughter of the couple you met at the parents' Welcome Week Roundtable for help. You know none of them would do all the things that you would, but you're not there. You want to rally the troops to come to your kid's aid.

Stop right there. Take a breath.

Our mothering instinct rages when our kids get sick or hurt. When every corpuscle pumping through your veins urges you to act, you feel the need to take control and start doing things. Stop. Calm the wave before it crashes into your lifeboat. You spent 18 years getting her ready for life on her own. She can survive a cold, the flu, fevers, infections, and strep throat. These will run her down, but not take her out. She will probably face them with a little less help and a little less coddling than she is used to. But she will survive.

16

Germs come and go. In most cases, you cannot do much besides make your son a little more comfortable, even if you were there. I'll admit, I learned this the hard way. I drove down to help my daughter get through a bad case of the flu (actual Influenza-A. You know, the really nasty one that knocks you off your feet for a week, the one the shots should prevent!) during her junior year. She needed someone to lean on to make it through the worst of it, and I had the flexibility to go, so I offered to come help. She kept getting sicker, and we were worried she would wind up in the hospital. Thankfully, she made it through.

Only after making the trip and heading home did I realize how little I actually did to help while I stayed with her. She spent most of the day sleeping, so we didn't spend much time together. As she recovered, she had no appetite, so I couldn't even prepare Mom's Home Cooking to help her feel better. I kept busy while she slept, scrubbing a neglected kitchen sink and disinfecting her bathroom in her apartment, and I made a run for groceries. But did she really need me there? No. She felt love and sympathy and encouragement, which was priceless at that moment, but it didn't change how sick she felt. Five days later, she was back at classes, and I drove back home. She recovered. End of story.

Would I do it again? In a heartbeat!

What can you do?

Prayers for Today

Pray for immunity when exposed to germs on campus, on every doorknob and in elevators and at shared desks.

Pray that your son's defenses activate and prevent the germs from taking root in his body.

Pray that other sick people do everything they can to keep their germs to themselves.

Pray for cleaning staff workers to be diligent in their efforts to disinfect common areas and equipment.

Pray for compassion and attention from friends who can step up and help during an illness.

Pray for quick healing for your daughter and restoration to full strength as soon as possible so work does not pile up.

Pray for a commitment to make up work and complete missed assignments so her grades do not suffer.

What else will you pray for?

4 You Can Do It. Yes, You Can!

Parents spend 18 years doing almost everything for their children. Sure, each time we give them a little responsibility or teach them a task, we add to their capabilities for adult independence. Assigning household chores teaches basic life skills. Handing your teenage son a list, $30, and two coupons at the front of a store pushes him along the path to savvy shopping. If your daughter wants to use the car, she has to learn how to pump gas at the station (and which station to pick, and to remember to take the debit card along).

We learn life's lessons in layers. No one gets a complete understanding of anything on the first attempt. The process involves trying, failing, comprehending, and growing. The same goes with taking on a new identity as a college student. Whenever they try something for the first time, they will realize their own shortcomings and uncover something that they have to do better the next time. It's an ongoing process.

Some parents refuse to give up their role as primary provider. They insert themselves into as many details of their child's life as they can. They manage schedules and commitments, then oversee coursework and study habits, and even hire tutors. Some of these parents contact coaches, provide weekly services like laundry and grocery delivery, and schedule transportation back home for regular visits. Even if you only do a few of these things, you may be in violation territory! Take a moment and think about how much you do to help your daughter. Helping them differs from helping them grow. Think about each task you still control and decide whether she would be better off learning how to do that on her own.

Now, please don't dump ten or twelve things on an unprepared college student all at once! They have four years to take on these new responsibilities. Try this instead: every time you start to handle something for your son, make a note about calling him to include him in the details. Walk him through the basics of what you do to accomplish it. If you've never exposed your daughter to choosing a flight and making a plane reservation, for instance, you can save her a lot of wasted effort by starting her with a brief explanation of travel websites and time requirements to consider when booking. Suggest that she ask her friends how they do it, too. They may have a resource which streamlines their efforts. If you don't explain the price differences depending on seat choice or travel day and time, you may find your daughter picks a very expensive Friday afternoon flight because it works the best with her schedule. An hour later could be $250 cheaper. It will be a learning experience. Another thing she might learn is that sometimes the best learning comes from hearing somebody else's experience and taking the advice they give based on what they have been through.

You didn't teach your son how to drive by walking him to the front of the car and saying, "Here's a key, now drive." You probably spent months talking to him while he was a passenger, covering things to pay attention to and how the gauges and systems worked. You explained the rules of the road. Maybe you pointed out how other drivers made risky moves and what your new driver had to do instead. You talked about how to adjust the seat and the climate controls to make the ride more pleasant. Then, you took the passenger seat and only guided when your new driver needed a little help. Sending your kid to college should happen the same way. Instead of dropping them at the door and saying, "Go be an adult now," parents should offer to be a resource for guiding them along in their learning process. Sure, they can probably make it on their own without too many crashes, but their life journey may need a parental GPS adjustment once in a while.

As you move from provider to advisor, remember that another important role you can take on is cheerleader. Too many students never hear any positive things from their parents. They receive a constant stream of questions, complaints, and criticisms. Their parents realize they are having fewer conversations, so they don't want to waste any time on anything but the important stuff. Think about it for a minute: would you want to take calls from someone who gives you a five minute interrogation and complaint-filled rant? I don't suggest sugar-coating discussions or avoiding the tough stuff, but make a deliberate attempt to balance your talks by asking about things that matter to them, and staying positive about the things they've learned to do on their own. Your encouragement during the hard times can motivate them to keep moving things forward. Give them a little boost, especially when they're not expecting it!

Two moms told me about a great talk that a college minister gave to an audience of parents on Family Weekend. He offered to share the closing of his inspiring message by including it for you here: "You're transitioning roles now, Moms and Dads. You're making a move into new territory. You used to be the waymaker with the sacred map, choosing every step for your kid as they grew up. They were the inquisitive passenger along for the ride, learning a little at each stop.

"Now, things have changed. You've passed along the map reading responsibilities to your kids. They're moving into adulthood. They get to choose the way to go now. You may get to be a passenger for a portion of the journey, but they may not even ask you to come along for the ride! They may choose to abandon your map completely and use a fancy GPS to guide them. They may go left when you've always, always, *always* gone right. But hopefully, they'll send you some postcards along the way as they go. They may even call for a little clarification of a destination. They might ask to see your old trip photos and share some of their new ones with you. Just realize it's not your journey to direct anymore! Step away from the steering wheel and let them drive. They'll get there by going their own way."

What can you do?

Prayers for Today

Pray for opportunities to give advice and suggest things as your son faces new challenges.

Pray for patience to let your daughter figure things out when she encounters roadblocks and dead ends.

Pray for reminders to encourage your son about completing smaller goals along the way to bigger accomplishments.

Pray for clarity in your new role, both in reacting to the new boundaries and in finding better ways to support them.

Pray for your daughter's desire to take over the wheel now and drive down her own path.

Pray that you move into the passenger seat willingly and ease into the transitions ahead with an open mind.

What else will you pray for?

5 College Costs Money, Mom

Tuition. Room and Board. Those are the basics. Now add Books. Fees. Transportation. School Supplies.

The college brochures suggest you put that amount in the budget for the "Real Cost of College." That total might get you onto campus.

But where do shampoo and Kleenex get added in? Or the $27 monthly charge for upgrading your daughter's cell phone data plan? How about the $19 entry fee for the campus charity dance-a-thon (and the $5 per hour you pledged)? What about the extra bookshelf and laundry basket your son needs to buy for the dorm room? How about the cost of gasoline, and the parking permit, and the parking tickets, and the $33 to get the inside of the car cleaned when your daughter drove four friends back to the dorm after the "Color Run"? (If you don't know what one is, Google it and look at the pictures.) Let's not even try to add up the coffees, smoothies, and snacks available in just about every building where students take classes.

The money goes out. And keeps going. Signing up for a sport or pledging into Greek life can obligate your student to thousands of dollars more in expenses. Travel costs beyond getting your son from home to school and back again add up, too (think basketball games, spring break, research presentations, volunteering, retreats, competitions, visiting friends at other schools, interviews…).

It's easy to say, "We want you to learn and grow, so try all kinds of new things at college." When the price tags add up, that sentence will not come out as easily. And for many parents, the realization hits hard: what they put aside as "Money to Use Later" disappears in the first two months, but the requests keep coming.

You don't want your son to worry about every penny. You also don't want him to spend on every whim. Try to strike a financial balance somewhere between doing it all for your daughter and making her figure it all out on her own. When your son tells you about facing a spending decision, ask him what he considered when he chose what he did, and offer some real-world advice or an experience which helped you learn how to get through a similar choice. Some kids won't listen to a word of it. Others will let a little seep into their brains and might use a bit. The desperate ones will ask for your help directly and want to back away from the financial mess they have created. Living an independent college life means different things when it comes down to real dollar signs.

No one looks forward to conversations about finances and money flow. You still need to have them. When the budget breaks, the spending has to stop. For many families, that means they have no more money to give. If you have set clear limits for your son and he spends beyond them, you can justify some harsh consequences. Unless your son earns it himself at that point, he will have nothing.

You may be part of a growing group of parents who challenge their students to set out as independent young adults from their first day on campus, sole providers for their existence from that point forward through the rest of their college careers. Taking on the responsibility for the costs of getting an education, these students juggle jobs and businesses as they earn their degrees. They often take longer than four years to do it, but some consider their real-life experiences more valuable than living the "college lifestyle" for that time. They realize the true priorities of providing for their own basic needs. It may be a harsh drop-kick into the realities of life, but it teaches some valuable Life Lessons.

Money is a perpetual topic for college students and their parents. No other time in life has such clearly delineated costs and unknown expenses at the same time. It's a good time for emerging adults to have discussions, listen to explanations, and learn the basics that will provide a firm foundation for the rest of their lives.

What can you do?

Prayers for Today

Pray for your daughter's decisions, that she can mindfully choose the ways she wants to spend money.

Pray for clarity in pursuing the right opportunities to prevent wasting money along the way.

Pray for clear Life Lessons which your son accepts and understands regarding spending choices.

Pray for wonderful role models to influence your daughter's choices.

Pray for wise use of the funds you have, whether you hand them over or continue to manage them.

Pray for continued provision of income to meet their college obligations.

Pray for awareness of resources to reduce your daughter's costs, like grants or scholarships, which can be unexpected blessings along the way.

What else will you pray for?

6 Praying for Them Through Tragedies

The text said: **NEED to talk to you NOW!

When that message came through on my phone, I shuddered. This did not sound like my daughter. Before I could type a word to reply the phone rang in my hands.

"Mom. Sit Down."

I couldn't choose to sit or respond fast enough, she just continued.

"Mom. Laurel's Dead. She died last night, Mom!" and then the rest of her words became an incomprehensible jumble of sobs and tears over the phone.

What could I say? One of her closest friends from high school had died? No words mattered.

When she stopped, I asked gently, "What happened? Who told you?" The facts managed to come out a little easier. Another friend had just called her with the news.

This can't be real, I thought. They had just gone to lunch together a month ago, right before school started.

Laurel had fought cancer during their high school years. She had gone into remission and started college just like the rest of their graduating class. She made it through the first year and was set to start year two. My daughter flew back home that August to spend a few weeks with us after a busy summer away, so before school started, she and Laurel met up to have some fun and spend some time together. As the new semester began, Laurel felt something wasn't right, and a few weeks later went back to the hospital to figure it out. They quickly determined her cancer had returned, so they scheduled her for another surgery. Without telling many people, she went back in, ready for another battle. She was set to fight again, and she looked forward to earning her own "Remission Accomplished" T-shirt like the one she saw on display in the hospital lobby. But complications developed, and she passed away within a few days of her surgery.

And this blindsided my daughter.

For two days, she lived in her own personal grief bubble. No one else she encountered shared her sorrow. No one on that campus had known her friend from home. No one consoled her or related her mood to the tragedy within her. She struggled to discuss it with friends who never knew Laurel and who had no reason to be aware of her grief. Hearing reactions like, "Oh, that's so sad!" or "I couldn't even imagine that," did not provide compassion for her loss or help her process her feelings. I wasn't there to stand by her through this. So I prayed for her. But my prayers could not make her world any better, and they could not bring her out of the trial she faced alone.

My daughter's campus offers grief counseling services, and a visit there started the process of informing her professors with an Official Approved Excuse to miss classes. That also allowed her to have special accommodations to make up missed quizzes and assignments which would not have been accepted late. But it also required sharing her feelings, at a very vulnerable time, with a stranger who had no connection to the friend she lost.

She grew up a lot that week.

No matter how hard we try to prevent the hard parts of life, they still happen. Some hit from out of the blue, even after years of knowing that they might happen sometime soon. The people who knew Laurel watched her low points and high points, knowing death was at her door more than once. But no one expected it on that September day.

We never know when the buzzer is going to ring as someone calls, "Time's up." No matter how unfair our kids feel it is, they can't control it. We can't control it either. People deal with loss differently each time they experience it. We handle some deaths we hear about at an emotional distance, with appropriate sorrow and condolences. Other losses are life-changing and life-challenging. Some college students have experienced losing many family members and friends throughout their lives. For others, their first experience with the death of a loved one or friend may happen when they are on their own at college. Either way, they will face new struggles as they learn to live with the reality of their loss.

I hope you won't need to find counseling services on your campus, but know that they are there if you need them. If a quick search doesn't lead you to the right support services, call the Office of Student Affairs or even the Residence Hall Director's office and ask for some assistance. They will get your son or daughter to the right people who can help.

What can you do?

Prayers for Today

Pray for protection from tragedies.

Pray for the ability to react calmly when your child's life turns upside down.

Pray for the safety and health of your daughter's friends, classmates, and extended family.

Pray for considerate responses from people around your son when he talks about the tragedies.

Pray for the words used by others to be caring, sensitive, and relevant as your daughter processes her loss.

Pray for the families of those living through tragedies to stay strong and supportive.

Pray that anyone going through the grieving process finds the support services they need to walk through this time of adjustment in their lives.

What else will you pray for?

7 I Know the Address

You drop your son at the dorm. You take a photo of the arched doorway. You mark it on the campus map so you have a visual reference point. You memorize the names of buildings to the left and the right, and you note the closest street names in all four directions. This is where he will be for the next year.

Well, not exactly.

If you take a moment and glance at the rest of the campus map, you will find a hundred other places he might be. On large campuses, that might grow to a thousand. If you're lucky enough to be standing on the campus of Texas A&M or Ohio State, you've just rubbed elbows with upwards of 60,000 other students. Those campuses have hundreds of dorms, classrooms, and facilities where your daughter can spend her time. She may get lost more than once, or probably more often than she will admit. Many college parking lots post reminders to users to "Note your specific lot number and location to assist you in retrieving your vehicle," since visitors get confused about where they've parked after walking across acres and acres on campus.

In simple terms, it is a big place. Students can roam, explore, find favorite spots, and designate areas they prefer to avoid. They decide if they will walk the direct routes or escape the crowds on side paths. When they need to cross campus, they will use trolleys and shuttles, or even buses and subways. When they attend events, they may need to use public transportation to reach additional campus facilities, sometimes close by and other times across a major city.

College campuses have grown bigger than you imagine. You can't see it all, you can't know it all. Even second-semester seniors with seven school terms under their belts still need to look up building locations when their new classes start. It will never be completely familiar. When we visited our daughter at the end of her summer seminar, we overheard two professors talking about the problems they had getting to the group's Poster Presentation. After thirty years on the campus, the first professor relied on his general understanding of where the building was and how to get there. He said, "I could see the top of the building and just headed for it. But the closer I came, the harder it was to keep it in perspective when other buildings nearby blocked it from view. Then I had to go around a fenced parking lot and around a dorm that I could not enter. The construction zones around the new Informatics building made things more complicated, too. And there just aren't any regular rectangular buildings anymore. Walking along the side of one, I realized I would have a long detour around two more wings before I headed in the right direction again. So, as the crow flies, it should have taken me ten minutes. But on this campus, it took me over 45 minutes to walk here!"

If the veteran faculty members can't even do it, then remind your daughter it will take time for her to get comfortable with all the new locations. Campus Freshmen will tell you they start out with a home base and a few landmarks. They judge locations in relation to the few places they know. They may waste a little time walking an indirect route across campus to re-align with a stable landmark. They may use the tallest buildings to set their mental compass to get to a new location. They also travel in larger groups to get to events. Some say it's just for the companionship, but most want the security of groups who can navigate them through the unfamiliar areas of campus. It will slowly become more familiar. Their comfort zone will gradually stretch to new areas they didn't even know existed.

Each day, as your son has new experiences on campus, a few more places will show up on his mental map. Your daughter will learn how to cut five minutes off of her walk by finding a shortcut through a building. College students master the bus stops and shuttle routes to get to classes across campus. They will find the best parking lots and learn the quickest exits from them. They figure out how to find their way even when they don't know exactly where they are going or how to get there. It's all part of Living the College Life.

What can you do?

Prayers for Today

Pray for safe transportation on campus as your daughter walks, drives, and rides.

Pray for the weather to have a minimal impact on your son's travels.

Pray for other drivers to be alert and maintain control while on campus.

Pray for safe commutes for your daughter's professors, the campus staff, other students, and visitors.

Pray for your son to develop a good internal compass to give him confidence in his travels around unfamiliar areas of the campus.

Pray for your daughter to develop her ability to understand directions in relation to things she is familiar with in finding her new destinations.

What else will you pray for?

8 The Sounds of Silence

Can there really be a story to tell about silence? You may be surprised.

Life is quiet now. It wasn't always, though. When your daughter was four, she never stopped talking. She spoke to everyone. Her sixth-grade teacher called her a future all-American debate winner. The girl liked telling the whole world what she knew. Having her in carpool challenged your friends' patience and sanity as they drove. Her probing questions forced them to look at the world in ways they never explored before, thanks to her perspective on things (which she shared all the time). She just wouldn't stop chattering.

But now, she is a college student. Every day you wait for the phone to ring. It never does. You check frequently throughout the day for emails or texts. Nothing. You send notes, letters, postcards, and packages. No acknowledgements. You leave open-ended text questions; you try multiple choice queries; you even resort to asking for a confirmation that she is still alive! Well, that one might get a three-word text reply: "I'm fine. Busy."

A friend shows you how to turn on "Read Receipts" so you can find out when she sees your texts. At least that confirms they arrive. You see occasional Instagram or Twitter posts which verify she's still conversing with someone this week. You decide that Caller ID and the ability to screen calls are the worst things ever designed. You scan Campus Life posts and event photos to catch a glimpse of your AWOL child. You're ready to send "Have you seen this missing person?" posters to her dorm director.

There might be an easier way.

After almost five weeks of silence, one mom sent a text to her son: "If you're not using this phone any more I'm turning it off. It costs too much money every month." That got an immediate response.

"What do you mean? I use it all day long!" her son sent back.

"Well, you never return my calls or texts. I thought you had stopped using it," she replied.

"Mom, I'm in class all the time. You always text when I'm busy. When I'm not, I'm texting other people on this phone. It's the only way to talk to other people. I need a phone."

"I'm glad you understand how it works. Since you never called or texted back, I assumed there was some new way to communicate on campus and you didn't need it anymore. So, if you can find time to text your friends, you can find time to respond to me, too. Otherwise, it gets turned off. Understood?"

She had to assume he understood. He did not respond.

Good job, Mom! Great approach! Give your daughter a reasonable amount of time to reply, considering her schedule and activities. If the time passes and she fails to respond, doing something a little drastic might restart the conversation. Just don't cause a panic attack with whatever you choose to say.

Trying an unexpected approach adds a stun-factor into an ongoing challenge. Use something shocking when you need it.

What can you do?

Prayers for Today

Pray for open, willing communication between you and your college student.

Pray for the mutual understanding of your expectations and needs.

Pray for using the right words to ask better questions, getting more responses and enhancing your conversations.

Pray that your son sets his own time limits for using social media and news feeds.

Pray that your daughter spends more time in face-to-face communication with friends.

Pray for a change to your son's preference for texting and commenting on posts over speaking verbally to anyone, even you.

What else will you pray for?

Don't let the silence continue. I would love to hear from you on my blog, Life As A College Mom 101. Read a little, ask some questions, share a story, and join into the conversation with other moms who know the challenges college students face. Take a look at:

www.lifeasacollegemom101.wordpress.com

9 Works Well with Others

In this world of collaboration, colleges have accepted the idea that students should get some experience working in teams. Science experiments can require multiple lab partners to create linked reactions and measure results. Business professors assign group projects where students with a variety of majors work together, using their individual field knowledge to support a strategic business project. History discussions use team analysis of many past events to identify patterns and impacts across different eras.

Remember the acronym TEAMwork? Together Everyone Accomplishes More work. That's the driving force behind all these group projects. If everyone does their unique part, the team can combine efforts toward reaching the final goal. College group assignments introduce members to working together as teams while they designate responsibilities, cover focus areas, and eliminate repetitive efforts. It's a useful way to handle a topic. Researchers have uncovered that you can "learn" some things by accepting the performance and results which someone else on your team produces. By combining your efforts with another team member's work, you both can be farther ahead.

Well, that's how it works in the perfect world. Then there's this scenario:

> Here in the real world, some team members lack equal motivation, effort, and capability to produce results. In College Life 101, this is the rule, not the exception. Your daughter might put in hours of work preparing for a group project meeting, only to find that her partners did not prepare at all. One member forgets to show up, another member had other things to do and has nothing ready, and a third took an unexpected approach that the rest of the group

rejects. After discussing their next steps, the project gets dumped on your daughter, "since she already did such a great job on her section." The others decide they can work on the oral presentation after she finishes writing, since they have schedule conflicts and other papers due and can't meet again. After the meeting, no one responds to her repeated texts requesting their help on the balance of the assignment.

You grumble about commitments when she tells you. You want to roll your eyes and shout, "Don't let them do that!" With the deadline looming and the disregard they've shown her, she feels she can't risk letting the project ride and forcing them to step up. She has no leverage over them. So, she writes the rest of the report. She sends it to the group and spells out, "I'm going to cover Section C. You will do all the rest. You need to include these things and create the graphs on your own. We only get one chance to do this, so it had better be right!" With the completed work in hand, now her partners find lots of time to discuss what they want to say. They expect your daughter to be there, too. She refuses. She has put too much time into it already, and she has another meeting to attend. They offer to wait until she's done or meet later at night, to prepare together. She repeats, "I'm going to prepare my part. Don't worry about mine and don't try to cover it in your part. You need to figure out the rest. I have time an hour before class to meet for a quick run-through. I'll see you then."

The story goes on... and it would end something like this: They gave the presentation. It wasn't stellar, but they received a good grade. When the professor and class asked questions about the report, your daughter fielded almost all of them. She conducted an impromptu demonstration based on the questions and then pulled together the conclusions. The group succeeded with your daughter carrying about 90% of the load.

But don't lose heart. Here's what might happen: One of the Post-Doc assistants who watched her presentation stops your daughter later that week. He asks if she has any interest in joining a research team. Her efforts and contributions to the project were clear. She knew her stuff. She's the kind of person they've been looking for.

Group projects can turn bad, or they can be spectacular. With the right participants and clear responsibilities, team efforts can change the world. Hope for the best!

What can you do?

Prayers for Today

Pray that your son's group members work well together.

Pray for balanced work expectations and efforts.

Pray for the synthesis of the project and for achieving their goals.

Pray for wise counsel as differences occur during the project.

Pray for personality conflicts and partner irritations to stay minimized.

Pray for good leadership and mentoring among the team members.

Pray for successful presentations that show the effort of the group.

What else will you pray for?

10 He Locks the Classroom Door

"Hello, Mom?" he starts our chat.

"Hi. Why are you calling now? Shouldn't you be in class?"

"Yeah, I should. But I can't get in," he tells you.

"What do you mean? Why not?"

"I didn't get here on time. I can't go in now."

"You can't miss class. Just go in quietly and take the first open chair. After class, stop and apologize for being late."

"I can't. I can't get in at all. He locks the door after he takes attendance so no one can come in after he starts class. He told us he doesn't like being interrupted when he's lecturing. What should I do?"

"Good Question! Never be late again?!?"

Some college professors treat their classrooms and labs as their own personal kingdoms where they reign supreme. They tolerate students as a necessary evil in their tenured world. On Day One, they instruct students on all the requirements of coexisting in their domain. Nothing is negotiable. Final grades depend on adherence to the rules as much as passing exams. Whether your student likes it or not, this is the way the ball bounces in this professor's class. For those 55 minutes, the professor makes all the rules, and can extract heavy penalties from lawbreakers.

Some professors make their time in the classroom more personalized. They like interacting with college students in every class. These instructors rank higher on most students' satisfaction scales, but their

39

style is not for everyone. They grade on curves, hold open discussions instead of lecturing non-stop, require little outside reading, make class attendance optional, and let students drop one test grade and one quiz from their final average. But if you're not the communicating type, you won't fit in well in these classes. Which would you choose, a professor from group 1 or group 2?

Most incoming students create their first schedule based only on course names and available time slots. They don't know any of the professors or how different they may be. Many freshmen find themselves stuck in rough classes their first semester. Those classes are still available after all the current students fill out their schedules because no one wants to take them. Professor reputations and stories about in-class experiences spread across the student body during class registration. Students talk about which professor to take for a class, or how certain teachers use tougher grading scales. Two sections of the same class, taught by different professors, can have completely different workloads:

Section 1: Professor A:	Section 2: Professor B:
4 Exams, Weekly Quizzes, Cumulative Final	3 Non-cumulative Exams; last counts as final
2 Research Papers	No Research Paper
2 group projects with poster presentations	1 group or individual project
Daily class participation included in grade	Extra Credit worksheets available
Recommends purchase of Study Guide and using department tutors for test prep	Group Study Sessions and Review Sheets available for test prep
Office Hours by appointment only. Teaching Assistants field all questions on material covered. Reminds students not to send anything to his department email because he never uses it.	Office hours available and instructor's personal cell phone number given to all students to use other times. Emails encouraged, and responds to texts usually within 4 hours.

Parents can argue the benefits and drawbacks of either approach. Does one teach better life skills? Does one class create a better person in the long run? Your son will complain about each class and professor he takes at some point, no matter which type he has. Your daughter will compare the workload she has with the workload of someone in another section. She'll think they get an easier ride. The grass is always greener on the other side of the fence. It doesn't matter what anyone else has to do; all that matters is what your student needs to do. Remind them of that. That's the Life Lesson. Then, after surviving it, your son will get to share some of his experiences with other students when the inevitable question comes, "What do you know about this class and this professor?"

What can you do?

Prayers for Today

Pray for a clear understanding of class expectations.

Pray about each class in your son's schedule, that he completes the requirements and takes every opportunity to learn in that classroom.

Pray for perseverance through the tough times in difficult courses.

Pray for selecting the best classes and professors matched to your daughter's learning style and strengths.

Pray for development of life skills throughout challenging courses.

Pray for respectful interactions with faculty and staff.

Pray that your son will get to know his professors outside of class and use them as resources and mentors throughout his time in college.

What else will you pray for?

11 It's a Job

The financial aid director told your son to look at the postings for on-campus employment to start earning his work-study award. If he does not put in the hours, he will not get the money. He looked. He did not find anything that he liked. He did not find anything interesting to him. They have 137 listings.

He does not want to work in the library and will not work in food service. He's not the type to lead new-student tours as a talkative Admissions Office ambassador. Okay, cut out all those and that still leaves 74 jobs on the list. 74 terrible jobs, Mom. None of them can compare to the job his friend found. That guy sits in a room signing out audio-visual equipment to professors.

"What's so appealing about that?" you ask.

"Think about it, Mom. Who uses AV equipment anymore? All the professors have their lectures on their computers. They just plug their laptops into the screens at the front of the room and go. Anything they want to show, they find on the internet and hit play. No one uses overheads or film projectors or slides except the old professors, or maybe one time during a semester when there's some really rare thing they can't find with a Google search. But this guy gets paid to sit there, three hours a day, three days a week. He just sits and studies and reads. If four people come in, it's been a busy day. And maybe that will take fifteen minutes, tops. He makes $10 an hour to sit and do his homework!"

Lucky kid!

Typical campus jobs do not show up on many people's "Top Ten Things I Want To Do for the Rest of My Life" lists. Most qualify as entry-level jobs and take basic skills. Depending on the job, your son might spend every minute engaged in a task, like lifeguarding at the campus swimming pool or teaching exercise classes in the gym. Other students find desk jobs in departments which have varying workflows and responsibilities every day. Answering phones in one department may mean a never-ending barrage, like in the Admissions Office, while in another they would only answer five an hour. Lab jobs vary in involvement, too. Some require doing the dirty work of washing beakers and cleaning petri dishes, others assign data input or computer analysis, and others require active data collection and direct involvement for extended periods with hands-on experiments or field studies.

Students get paid for their time and their effort. Your daughter will take a job and show up for it because she gets a paycheck at the end of the week. (That paycheck has to be worth the effort in the long run, though.) She does not need to have other goals associated with doing this job. She is obligated to show up, and her boss will be obligated to pay her for satisfactory work. You tell her there's more to working than that. Maybe your son wants the cash. You want to see him grow through the experience. Isn't that what college life is all about, anyway? Following through with taking a job, making a commitment to perform, being evaluated, and learning to work with others will all help his character develop. If your student wants experience but needs more flexibility in his commitment, the campus may offer plenty of opportunities to volunteer. Volunteering involves doing something for no pay that makes a difference for someone or some greater good. Many volunteer opportunities teach the same Life Lessons that regular employment teaches, with varying levels of commitment.

If your son has never had a job, be ready for the trials of taking on this new responsibility. Students who worked during high school might have already mastered showing up for work, being on time, making transportation arrangements and checking bus schedules, preparing uniforms, following a dress code, or bringing equipment. Or, any of these might be new concepts. Every job has unique expectations and requirements, so past experience does not equal preparation. This same position may require a learning curve under a new supervisor in another setting. Things will be different there.

Jobs take effort, time management, communication, and self-evaluation. Some require additional responsibility outside of work for maintaining personal equipment, uniforms, or tools. Your son may need to manage extra training time or preparation for daily assignments beyond his scheduled shifts. Some jobs involve cooperation with coworkers and submission to authority. They might lead to missteps or failures, with criticism and poor reviews from managers. They may require more effort than originally expected. Showing up for work may mean less study time, social time, or time for other activities. Their obligation to working their scheduled shifts may mean they will miss out on something they really want to do. That's a Life Lesson they need to learn and experience. Your daughter needs to stay committed through all the ups and downs. It's all part of the job.

Let the balancing begin.

What can you do?

Prayers for Today

Pray for the balance between life as a student and life as an employee.

Pray for finding a job that matches your son's needs, interests, and time commitments.

Pray for full awareness of expectations and responsibilities.

Pray that your daughter will find a position matched to her capabilities that offers opportunities to grow.

Pray for safety as your son works in his campus job. Also pray for the safety of other student workers across campus.

Pray for learning and life awareness from experiences which help develop their career choices.

What else will you pray for?

12 On the Team

Many college students depend on a sports scholarship to pay for their tuition. Without it, they wouldn't be on campus. College sports teams across the country recruit thousands of prospective students every year. They offer scholarships to cover full or partial tuition, and throw in travel expenses, training fees, and many other costs awaiting the entering freshman. By accepting the scholarships, these students commit to taking a role on the team or in the sport. They will also take on the identity of "Athlete," which will give them responsibilities and privileges across campus. From that point on, their schedule will always need to accommodate games, meets, travel, practices, and conditioning. Everything else on their schedules moves to lower priority, including classes, activities, jobs, homework, family obligations, and campus events (… and even their sleep).

Traveling athletes who regularly leave campus for matches and tournaments may have their class schedules created by specialized advisors who know their availability and time conflicts. Athletes often get priority for class spots because they can't risk "waiting list" schedule disasters. Team members who train early in the morning get special access to food service and conditioning facilities outside of regular operating hours. Special advisors and counselors work with athletes who miss classes for events, arranging alternate due dates and substitute work plans. Most of the professors have no say in the matter; their willing accommodation is expected.

By taking an athlete identity, these students live a different life than the ones their friends live. They have high expectations put on them on the sports field, but often there are lower ones put on them for academics. Some get capped at taking 3 or 4 courses during their competitive season, due to their time commitments. Others must agree to taking summer courses so they can still graduate on time. All these accommodations lead back to the basic thing you need to realize: sports take time, and you can't use that time to do anything else.

Your son may make an amazing contribution to his team. He may develop leadership skills and attain personal goals. He may be named Player of the Year. Your daughter may find new ways to balance life's demands while striving toward unmet dreams and better personal performance. She may learn a new understanding of encouragement and motivations. She might win Best Athlete accolades. Bravo!

Unless they plan to continue playing their sport or have a career in sports management, they might need a rebalancing at some point. It often happens unexpectedly after an injury sidelines them from competing. As they watch from the bench, all the people they identify with, especially teammates and coaches, move on without them. Losing their spot to participate, they may face the hardest identity crisis of their lives. The worst may come when a major injury forces them to face the premature end of their college sports career. Unfortunately, when many injured college athletes lose their connection to the team, they find remaining at the same school too painful and decide to leave.

A mom shared this story: My son took a full ride scholarship to play Division 1 football. He spent the entire summer before freshman year conditioning and in training camps. He made the team, but only had three minutes of game time his first year. He needed to watch and learn, they told him. He was training 15 hours a week or more. Because he was on the team, he had caps put on his class schedule and only carried 11 credits his first semester. When trying to schedule for Spring semester he found that he couldn't take most of the business courses he wanted or needed. Either they weren't offered or they had prerequisites which he hadn't taken yet. For Spring he settled on an English, a History, a Sports Conditioning class and a Science with a lab. None of them would do any good for his Business School major, but they filled core requirements.

He spent his next summer in training camps again. We only saw him once for a weekend visit home. He said it mattered to the coaches for him to be there every day, to make sacrifices and show that being part of the team meant something to him.

That fall, we watched his first pre-season scrimmage, in the rain, ready to see him play. He didn't get called in until the 4th Quarter. On his third play, he was in the wrong spot at the wrong moment when an opposing teammate lost footing on the wet field during a tackle. This 250-lb lineman came crashing down on my son's leg, pushing his knee into an ugly angle and then snapping his shin bone in two places. No one needed to see the instant replay.

After surgery and almost a week in the hospital, my son decided that his semester was pretty much over. He knew he was never going to be part of the team again. He couldn't see the point of struggling to get to any of those classes he didn't want to be in, and juggling physical therapy sessions and off-campus doctor appointments with no car and no one to drive him. (College independence has its perks until you need to be able to depend on someone!) He withdrew from classes and came home.

Fall turned into winter, and we talked about his options for getting back to school. He had no desire to go back. He took a part-time job near home and agreed to take a few courses at the local branch of a state college. His recovery took a long time, and so did his education, but he managed to finish a degree in Human Resource Management and now has an HR position with a Fortune 500 company. It's definitely not the path we thought he was destined to take. Life has a way of surprising you sometimes and shaking things up. You need to deal with whatever comes.

Other types of sports-related pressures cause rebalancing, too. Sometimes a losing season makes the path seem a little less rosy. Some athletes get a reality check when younger players move past them to fill prime spots in the lineup. Then the sport's sparkle begins to fade and your daughter might feel a part of her identity is cracking. Your son may begin making excuses for not working out or spending less time training, deciding it's just not worthwhile anymore.

Commitments are commitments, and they need to fulfill their obligations. Quitting the team may not be an option for another reason. Their entire college career may be in jeopardy if they depend on sports scholarships to pay for it. If their athlete identity fades, you may begin feeling a change in perspective on the real costs of college.

What can you do?

Prayers for Today

Pray for your daughter's strength and endurance to meet the demands put on college athletes.

Pray for coaches and advisors who will balance your son's personal development with goal achievement.

Pray for humble winners who encourage the defeated to keep growing.

Pray for clean competitions, especially for protection from injury, cheating, and unfairness, and for impartial officials and judges to oversee them.

Pray for an honest evaluation of the role that sports will play in your daughter's life.

Pray for reasonable expectations from the trainers and coaches as they work with your son and his teammates.

Pray for your son's awareness of how to enjoy participating in sports and keep school goals in focus at the same time.

What else will you pray for?

Check-In Time

Have you been praying at the end of each chapter so far? Have the **Prayers for Today** helped you pray about some things that impact your college student right now? Did you shift your prayer style away from using Blanket Prayers, and move to specific prayers that have a connection to your daughter's or son's daily life? Let me know about it by commenting at: **lifeasacollegemom101.wordpress.com**

And keep praying!

13 Sometimes the Door Opens.
Sometimes It Shuts.

In the grand scheme of things, the four years spent in college during the typical 80+ years of life add up to less than 5% of the time an average human lives on earth. So, it's not such a big deal, right?

Wrong, mom.

The college years establish your life's stepping stones. These can set the pathway to first jobs, relationships, life choices (such as the city you'll move to), and personal responsibilities. Every day brings another new idea which could impact your daughter's future choices. Those new ideas unsettle her current satisfaction level about what she has already decided, and can send her rolling in a new direction. Your son will uncover new career fields to explore beyond the ones he knows about now. His path may veer off course to the left and seem to get lost in an overgrown forest. He may decide to pursue something which neither of you had even heard about before. That means there won't be a clear road visible up ahead, and making his way won't be easy.

Once your student decides on a path to follow, they will find they have a lot of little decisions to make along the way. Door #1, Door #2, or Door #3? Taking this course fills a prerequisite for next year's preferred class options and opens that door. Taking another course makes your son more aware of his growing interest in another area of science, which starts closing his original door and popping up a new one to walk through. Not getting a spot in a full class closes a door and turns your daughter's curriculum plan upside down since it was the critical next step to take. Missing a deadline for an application shuts the door on an opportunity for a research project proposal, which limits your son's experience on his resume. Taking certain steps in specific order along the path matters, sometimes more than anyone understands until they have gone farther down the line. Only then do they find out that a door they want to use has a "No Admittance" sign.

All these things could impact your college student's plans. Doors open and doors close. Just identifying what's behind all the doors can become a full-time job during college. Opportunities abound, but they often get buried in the clutter. Nothing clearly directs your son's efforts to rank these options. The endless demands of "You need to do this," "Apply for these," "Submit that," and "Complete those," will overwhelm your daughter's schedule. No one has a connect-the-dots map which lays out the important life choices to stick to (and the ones to avoid which would take you away from the big picture).

Sometimes their big picture shifts out of focus for a while. That's okay. Your daughter needs time to explore her choices a little after deciding to change majors. She doesn't know what she wants to do with her life now. If your son spent the last ten years talking about being a politician, he needs a chance to readjust when he decides corporate accounting would make him happier.

That's when opening and trying out more of these doors can help your daughter. Your son needs to know it's okay to select a door, peek inside, drop in for a quick visit, and decide it's not right for him. Another 20 doors await. Some might seem like a waste of time, but they each play a part in sharpening your son's awareness of what's right for him. Considering the choices helps clarify which path your daughter should take. You may see her wheels spinning and watch her making only a little progress for a while, but each experience helps her grow a bit more.

What can you do?

Prayers for Today

Pray for a goal to work toward, to help identify which doors have significance.

Pray for options which build a solid path to follow.

Pray for your daughter's willingness to try new things when some attempts don't turn out well.

Pray that they will reflect on their experiences and find value in the parts they enjoyed even if they shift to another plan or life goal.

Pray for refocusing the big picture, that it happens quickly when needed and sets your son on a new road without much struggle.

Pray that the distractions which cloud your daughter's choices stay at a minimum, that the real value of options comes clear to narrow her view.

What else will you pray for?

14 Surrounded by a Good Group

Some colleges boast that their students can participate in hundreds of different student organizations on campus. Small campuses may have limited reach, but every college has a lengthy list of groups your student can join. Whatever their interests involve, they can probably find a campus-organized group which meets regularly that covers them. Anything from a Harry Potter Fan Club, to Social Justice Lobbying, to Intramural Pickle Ball, the list goes on and on.

If you look through the lists, you may find that your son's campus has partnerships with some religious organizations which run faith-based groups. These religious activities rarely get prime space in Student Union events or publications, so finding out about them can be difficult. Some campuses no longer give space to non-chartered religious organizations in Campus Activity Fair events, so long-standing groups get no exposure to new students. Their challenge in existing starts with establishing student awareness that they are there. If your daughter wants to find a faith-based group to join on campus, there are probably plenty. It may surprise your son to know the group sponsoring his free pizza and movie nights is a religious group which would welcome him to join them.

A few campus religious groups have affiliate chapters at colleges across the country. Campus Crusade for Christ and the Fellowship of Christian Athletes meet in groups on hundreds of campuses. Just let your son know they may only use the modified versions "Cru" or "FCA" as their name in their posts about upcoming events, or he might miss them. Your daughter might not recognize some very good groups with denomination roots if she has not heard of them before. RUF (Reformed University Fellowship) has 150 college chapters across the country staffed by pastors who connect with students at weekly worship meetings and in small group Bible Studies. They also encourage members to attend local churches within the neighboring community, often arranging carpools and rides. Since other religious groups' names aren't clear indications of who they are, finding out more about the purpose and beliefs of Intervarsity, Hillel, FOCUS, TriCycle, Young Life, the Navigators, Zen Med, YUVA, or Movement, can take extra effort by your daughter.

If your college does not have an Office of Campus Ministries or a Religious Life Department, the Admissions Office or the Office of Student Affairs can answer questions about which religious organizations she can find on campus. Sometimes students in those groups only use word-of-mouth invitations for upcoming activities that give new students the chance to try the group. If your son's effort to find a group hits a dead end, suggest an internet search using his college name and "religious groups" to uncover some new possibilities to contact.

Finding community and receiving encouragement from like-minded people builds a support mechanism for our college students. In this new world they're a part of, sharing a foundation built on similar beliefs helps them as they branch out to new ideas. Having a foothold in a religious group may steer your daughter's choices along a straighter path, as appealing new opportunities come into view. Getting regular exposure to other students who share similar values can encourage your son to maintain his faith walk. Connecting with ministry staff and counselors can provide advice and encouragement throughout rough patches during the semester. Through it all, your daughter will develop strong friendships with students she meets who share her faith.

What can you do?

Prayers for Today

Pray that each student who wants to participate in a religious group finds the right one.

Pray that your son stays open to grow in his faith.

Pray for your daughter to find friends who share her priority for following and sharing her convictions.

Pray for your son's connections with the Campus Ministry staff on a personal level, for mentoring and counseling resources.

Pray for the growth of the ministry to reach both students who have not yet committed to participate as well as students who need to find a good group like this.

Pray that the entire ministry stays shielded from outside influences and antagonism against religious groups on that college campus.

Pray that your son will avoid the attraction of radical movement groups which manipulate students' thinking and stifle free thought.

Pray that students who have rejected ministry outreach in the past will be open to an invitation for another event.

What else will you pray for?

15 Getting Past the Worry List Prayers

Everyone has been there: calling out to God for help in a crisis. We reach out for a last-minute life preserver. For some of us, sending urgent requests has become a common prayer tactic. That spills over into how we pray for our college students. We cry out with pleas to help our sons and daughters through their desperate moments.

God listens. He understands.

Here's something to consider: you enjoy having conversations with your daughter more often than just at the crisis moments, right? You like to hear the good things that have happened in your son's life and the new things he has tried. You like to hear that your daughter has accomplished things and what she plans to do next. God does too. Try to balance your conversations with Him between your needs and your thanks. It's easy to compile the List of Wants and Worries where you ask for intervention and direction. But parents often forget to include time for reflection and giving thanks for all that God provides. We cover the proud moments of our student's accomplishments with gratitude, but we neglect to recognize God's constant provision and sustaining grace.

Instead of filling your quiet time with desperate prayers for crisis moments, try balancing your prayer topics. Add prayer time for appreciation and time to pray for their everyday lives. Take a quick mental inventory of three areas: their activities, the people they interact with, and their basic needs day-in and day-out. Cover one or two of those areas each time you start praying. Next, add in your prayers for their maturity and continued growth. By asking for development of their character and their work habits as they connect with others on campus, you keep their needs center stage. Soon you may find yourself praying for their character qualities and personal growth more often than for an individual quiz grade. And which matters more for the rest of your student's life? Building them up in prayer throughout the quarter will help them more than a last-minute plea on the night before midterms.

If you have a chance, share with your son that you're praying for him. Mention some of these non-critical things you're including, and you may start him thinking about why you cover the small things, too. Hopefully that will activate his awareness for putting his needs into prayer.

Encourage your student to take time to pray, too. Sustained prayer can be calming when it helps to bring things into perspective and clarify priorities. Repeatedly praying for specific projects gives your son more time to evaluate his effort on them. Stepping back and analyzing the progress he has made, the work left to do, and ranking the importance of other deadlines against this work will give him a clearer priority list. If your daughter has a prayer routine, when the crisis moments happen, she will have a calmer reaction and a better understanding that she can process through the conflict and overcome the adversity she faces.

Make your prayers a priority every day. It's too easy for other things to get in the way in our busy lives. Use something you do regularly as a reminder to pray (like clearing the dinner table). Open your heart and deepen your awareness of God in your life. Ask for it to flourish in your son's life too. Spend time praying about your daughter's growth, to help her prepare for her future. Take the quiet time you need. It may give you a clearer understanding of the path ahead.

What can you do?

Prayers for Today

Pray for your transition from Worry Prayers to Everyday Prayers.

Pray for awareness of new prayer topics which would help build up your daughter.

Pray for your son's ability to handle difficulties, through growth and through learning to manage his priorities.

Pray for becoming aware of new ways to pray and deepening the conversation you have with God in prayer.

Pray for opportunities to share with your daughter how you're praying for her.

Pray for your son to encounter reminders to pray.

Pray that each student, especially yours, finds prayer helpful.

What else will you pray for?

16 Just Between You and Me

As your student makes strides in developing his independence, you may encounter an unexpected conflict on the home front. You may find that you and your spouse do not share the same approach in dealing with your emerging adult. Parents can watch children move away from home to college campuses and expect very different things about their involvement in decisions concerning the future. Hopefully, they have taken the time to have some deep discussions about real life and the college experience prior to move-in day. Even after setting some basic expectations and breaking down some communication barriers, your daughter may surprise you with her choices in the first few weeks of campus life. Your son may feel his new freedoms allow all the boundary-testing and experimenting he wants to try.

At some point, they will make some choices that you wouldn't. You find out and you feel disappointed. When you discuss this with your spouse, you might not find a concurring opinion. Instead, you get, "That's really not that bad. Think about the stuff that people did when we were in college." Something that you feel was a major misstep, since your "Danger" alarms are blaring, can seem trivial to another parent.

My suggestion: choose your battles.

Most of the time, a battle between parents over the decisions a college student makes will have no impact on whether or not their son continues doing what he's started doing. He's growing. He's becoming independent. Your daughter has opened up to influences and information from outside sources. That means the way it has always been may never be the same again.

So start from here. You and your spouse need to talk to each other about your expectations. Point out how your son's actions differed from them, and what you need to discuss with him to clarify your agreed-on stand. This will not be easy.

One parent wants to limit interfering, another wants to guide.

One parent offers money freely to enable life experiences, another wants to teach the value of the hard-earned dollar.

One parent has "Intolerables," the things which will not be permitted from any member of their household at any time, *Ever!*, and another wants to let their children learn from their own mistakes.

One parent wants to wrap their child in bubble wrap to prevent any potential injury, while another wants to find a Band-Aid after they fall, but only if they ask for one.

Instead of fighting with your spouse over your parenting style, try to air your opinions and resolve your differences in open discussions. Use a few "What if…?" questions to get a better understanding of how they want to handle future powder kegs. You won't always agree, and that's okay. One of the best things you can do is learn to take a moment to think before you respond. Some problems will knock you off base; try not to react immediately in anger or with disappointment. If you can, step away and hit reset before you try to fix the world. Sometimes you can be the strong one if your spouse is having a harder time processing the conflict. You each have different strengths and tolerances, so one of you may be more ready to deal with an issue than the other. The key is to move forward together when you can.

A little time to think gives you time to diffuse the emotions. Then you can get back to clearing up the differences you have with your spouse or with your student. You might work through a compromise to the current problem which combines both your own and your spouse's concerns. Another option would be to talk more with your son so you understand the reasoning behind his decision. Then you can think about his new perspective before choosing to pursue your position. Remember that you cannot make decisions for your daughter, but you can advise her on the pros and cons of any situation. Asking to talk about areas which worry you may provide the opportunity to bring up things your son did not consider when he made his choice. Be careful though: if you start with ultimatums, expect any listening to shut down and the arguments and frustration to follow.

What can you do?

Prayers for Today

Pray that you will always listen first before reacting.

Pray that your discussions will keep you ready to face the unexpected.

Pray for open minds and hearts in dealing with new ideas.

Pray for understanding of your spouse's viewpoint as differences arise.

Pray for productive compromises which put your daughter's needs at the forefront.

Pray for your son's acceptance of good advice and his willingness to consider your questions as he makes major decisions.

What else will you pray for?

17 People Have a Lot to Say

The Voice of Tomorrow lives on college campuses, influencing what students think and what matters to them. It undermines long-held beliefs, establishments, and reasonable political debate. It shuns labels and affiliations. It accepts everyone by accepting everything, except anyone whose ideas exclude someone. Stop and think about that for a minute.

The Voice of Tomorrow puts opinion in the driver's seat. It opposes systematized beliefs and historical facts. It teaches that all events have optional considerations which an observer can use to determine relevancy. A politician calls out, "Truth isn't truth. It's all relevant depending on your perspective." A church decides, "Old ideas were not inclusive, so we have rewritten our doctrine." A college professor in a popular movie states, "Your religious ideas are ridiculous and worthless. You will fail if you challenge me with them again." Influencers warn, "If you don't agree with the new thinking, the world will leave you behind."

Cultural shifts take hold on college campuses because students are in the process of making decisions about their beliefs. They grasp onto new ideas and listen to many viewpoints. Their expectations, values, and social ideals will morph into their individualized view of the world. Students use them to fuel their ideas of what their world should be. Lots of influences will create significant inroads and overpower what they already know. The new ideas challenge the intertwined bases of fact and reason that exist in their minds. College activists call out to them with open proclamations of controversial ideas, often silencing opposing sides as "intolerant." Their message is, "I have the right to say what I want, as loudly as I want, but you don't have the right to tell me things I don't want to hear."

Your daughter may avoid these debates and conflicts like the plague, until one day when she gets cornered outside her biology lab by students who oppose all animal research. They are "looking out for the innocents of the world," they say. "People have no right to do this," they say. But she knows her professor used the results he found from those animal experiments to give children with a debilitating disease the medicine they need to live past the age of two. They are dying without it. So, which is better? Which is right? Each side has their point.

Whether the topic covers politics, social justice, human rights, or governmental change, your son will hear persuasive pleas from very influential speakers on campus. Keeping an open mind might be difficult if he only gets to hear one side of the debate. Parents, get ready for some controversial ideas and some influenced conclusions to come your way.

What can you do?

Prayers for Today

Pray that your daughter will consider new ideas but will challenge them in her own mind as she listens to new opinions.

Pray for your son's friends to respect his opinions even if they disagree.

Pray for bold and persuasive speech against things which challenge your daughter's convictions.

Pray for your son to develop reasonable questions for people who share controversial ideas, to encourage their own consideration of their beliefs.

Pray for peaceful, safe, respect-filled interactions between opposing sides in these exchanges.

What else will you pray for?

18   The Phone Doesn't Work Like That

I heard this story from a mom: "I tried to call our son. His phone is disconnected. He had the responsibility to pay the bill. He has a job. I just don't understand how he messed this up." Besides shrugging your shoulders, what can you do?

I'm sure there was a conversation like this soon after that moment:

"Hi Mom."

"Hi! I almost didn't answer since I didn't recognize this phone number. Whose phone are you using?" she asks.

"A guy from class let me borrow his. My phone died. It just won't work anymore. And, yes, it's charged."

"Well, the message when I call says it's disconnected. They won't just do that for nothing. Did you pay your bill?"

"Yes. Well, I guess I did because it just takes money right out of my account every month," he said.

"Oh, okay. And your auto-payments have been going through okay?" you ask.

"Sure, why wouldn't they?"

"Well, things can go wrong, like not having enough money in the bank to cover the total?"

"Wait, what? How would I know if I have enough to cover it? I don't know how much it will be each time! They just take it out."

65

"We told you about this when you were setting it up at the bank. Your phone company sends you an email with your total charges about two weeks before it's due. Then you know how much you have to keep in your account to cover it."

"But what if I'm using that money?"

"Well, that's the thing. You can't use that money because it has already been spent on the phone and you don't get to use it on something else. So where did your paycheck go?"

"Well, I was going out to eat with people and I needed it, so I just cashed it instead of putting it into my account."

"Son, if you spend the money on other things, you can't pay your bills. You need to keep money in your account. The ATM is not a magic box that just prints the money you want when you want to use it. If you don't pay your bill, they turn off your phone. Do you understand now?"

"Not really. I mean I set up autopay — they're supposed to just pay it. I'm not going to keep working just to pay bills every month!"

"Actually, yes, you are. That's what you'll do every month for the rest of your life. And by not spending it all each month, you get to save some and then buy things you want to have. That's the story of life as an adult."

Another Life Lesson learned. (Probably with some hefty fees for the late payments and bank overdrafts. Tell your student about those, too.)

Money comes and goes. In our world of debit cards and autopays and paperless statements, we haven't exposed our kids to the realities of cash flow. Too many college kids hit campus with a minimal understanding of money. They have a debit card, and it shows their balance, so they spend it. Even if they had jobs before, they probably have never been responsible for bill payment or budgeting. If you were wise enough to expose your daughter to the realities of due dates and bank balances, there are tons of other loose ends you never would think to mention.

Be ready for a financial surprise. It will come. You hope that it won't make too deep a dent in your son's pocket, or in yours. One survey found seven out of ten college students pay at least one late fee or insufficient funds penalty during their campus years. Four out of ten students leave college with no understanding of their accumulated student loan obligations or credit card debt. Most say it happened because their parents had handled all the details for them prior to that point.

Every student has a different path to take in Financial Education. Some scrape by to earn every penny spent on their schooling. Others had bank balances in the six-figure range before they started college. No matter how they came in, they will need to learn some money management during their college years. Even when they head out on their own, you can still bring up money matters in conversations. Helping them stay on track will prepare them for big obligations and big decisions as they get through college.

What can you do?

Prayers for Today

Pray for wisdom in handling money, for patience in saving and for responsible spending.

Pray for awareness of financial obligations and capability in choosing, handling, and paying them.

Pray for growth in areas your daughter is unprepared for, which you may not even be aware of yet.

Pray for protection from greed, envy, pride, or other unhelpful attitudes toward money and the things people own.

Pray for quick relief from financial burdens when they arise.

Pray for awareness and quick understanding of new financial concepts.

What else will you pray for?

Have you talked about any of the Life Lessons mentioned in these chapters with your son or daughter? Share your story with other moms at:

www.lifeasacollegemom101.wordpress.com .

19 Answer These 10 Questions to Find the Perfect Roommate

Messy or Tidy? Stays up late or early bedtime? Study with music playing or in total quiet?

The college guidebook says these questions provide a match with a perfect roommate. Really? That's very funny!

Residence Life experts pair up incoming students to share dorm rooms. They face a daunting task. It must take a little ego, or maybe a little mojo. How can someone determine compatibility based on a handful of multiple choice questions? The truth hurts: they can't. The housing directors first weed out all the extreme answers and outliers they uncover. They match those people to similar souls at the start. Then everyone else becomes average. Each one can match to about 64 other people in their similar-preferences pile. Housing staff members make summary judgements on the likelihood a roommate pairing will succeed based only on avoiding things which past students have found most likely to cause conflicts. There's really not much mojo going on at all.

Lots of college students get along with their first roommate. Lots of others don't. Even when potential roommates fill out lengthy surveys and join chat rooms which operate like mini online dating sites, the merchandise you get doesn't always end up like the packaging or the advertising you've viewed. Living with a roommate is almost like marrying someone. You wouldn't let your daughter agree to marry a stranger after chatting with him three times and checking out his social media page. Yet, some people believe that's all you need to find a perfect roommate match. Will it be a marriage made in heaven? Probably not.

Even so, colleges bring all these incoming freshmen together into 1-year living arrangements "for better or for worse."

Learning to get along with someone new is a hard concept. In our social media and chatroom society, some college students approach friendships with a small packet mindset. They look for face value emotion and quick interactions. Since spending time with people involves more baggage than they want to take on, they avoid personal contact. They live in their own little worlds, drowning out their surroundings with their personal music choices in their noise-canceling earbuds. Their preferences reign supreme, and they can thumbs-down anything they dislike to show their disapproval and rally other similar-thinking friends around them.

Their approach to sharing a room and spending time with someone doesn't involve sharing. They expect to still be in charge of every element, because it's what they want. That's all that matters. Our world has changed from "share the experience and grow together," to "watch me do what I want and tell me you like it." That's a tough playing field for a college student trying to make the roommate concept work. Even having shared-effort experiences like team sports and membership in structured organizations does not develop cooperation anymore. Individuals focus more on their own grandstand moments and personal successes than on teamwork.

So, in this World of The Individual, how do new roommates get along? Not perfectly. Remind your son that his world overlaps with other people's worlds. Issues that seem black and white in the real world have lots of shades of gray in between. If your daughter has brothers or sisters, remind her how their lives and choices intertwined with hers while growing up in the same household. If your son was an only child, the time has come to reinforce that it's not all about him anymore. No one gets their preferences 100% of the time in real life.

Sharing a room for a school year with a new roommate will change your daughter. Even rooming with someone she knows will bring new challenges to a friendship. Hope for a good match and try to suggest ways your son can handle irritations and unmet expectations. Be ready to act as the sounding board for all the aggravations. Encourage your daughter to explore more options in finding a roommate when selections start for the next term. Sometimes students' prior disappointments make them apathetic about the chance of finding a good match. With a little outreach among friends and word-of-mouth referrals, your son might meet "a friend of a friend's lab partner" who also needs a new match for next year. Finding out about that person may make their next room sharing experience much better.

What can you do?

Prayers for Today

Pray that your son will be a good roommate and get a good roommate.

Pray for your daughter's confidence to share expectations and preferences while respecting her roommate's choices.

Pray for similar perspectives on what they each expect from a roommate.

Pray that each roommate will respect the other's need for quiet time, personal space, and privacy in the shared environment.

Pray that they encourage each other, enjoy their time together, and stay satisfied with their living arrangements.

Pray for the opening of these private bubbles of personal perspective to emerge into a world of shared living.

What else will you pray for?

20 The Procrastinator

Your college-aged son has not grown out of his habit of sliding through life on the verge of a deadline disaster.

Your daughter takes your phone call, only to tell you, "I can't talk. I have this paper due tomorrow and I still need to study for my German quiz and do my chemistry lab report."

Time management takes too much time, he tells you. She thinks she can't plan because there are too many variables in her life right now. She has no idea what might come up, so she needs free time in her schedule. All the reasoning makes complete sense to them, but it bewilders you.

Part of the blame may lie on you for this one, Mom. You shuttled him around from school to soccer practice, then to the library to pick up some things he needed for the science project and back home to a waiting dinner. You scheduled his life to work with yours, and with your other family members' lives, without ever explaining how you made it flow. If you never told your daughter that picking her up meant shifting grocery shopping to the next day, she did not understand the "choose one and move one" juggling you did every day.

I used to stare in awe and wonder at a friend's day planner. With five active kids and a job as a tutor, this lady had time slots micromanaged from before dawn until late into the night. She would whip out a different colored pen for each family member to add meetings, practices, and appointments. Like a drill sergeant, this friend planned household chores during her daily schedule with self-imposed time limits. When she had to add an unexpected tutoring student to the day, she often managed to carve out even more time from her packed schedule. She was awesome!

You would think her kids followed that fantastic system when they became adults, right? Wrong. My friend had such a system going, she didn't even think about how she planned things. Since she didn't think about it, she didn't talk about it, either. She did her mental juggling and made things work. But she never shared how she did it. Her kids couldn't even begin to understand how to shuffle and prioritize and make things fit. Plus, because their steps were directed in down-to-the-minute schedules, they didn't understand the process of planning, preparing, building in contingencies, estimating time commitments, and being ready to turn down one option when another option was more important. They did not even know that they had other options — their lives were packed full, and that's all they thought there was.

Many of our kids start college without having a great understanding about time management and choices. Your daughter wants to do everything that interests her and still manage a full course load and a part-time job. Your son will get disappointed when he hears about an event he missed, or a group he can't join because it meets at the same time as the other one he already joined. FOMO exists all over campus: Fear of Missing Out. Your daughter will want to add things to a packed day and then spend a good portion of the night cramming in work for her classes the next day. We won't even talk about the chronic lack of sleep!

The schedule and the to-do list need to live in perfect harmony, happily ever after. In most cases, they don't. Learning a planning method that works takes time. Your son may refuse to follow your system and balk at the idea of time commitments, but he'll soon find out he needs a plan to get through the busy days of his college career. Your daughter may pull plenty of all-nighters so she has time to go to every theatre presentation on campus this year. She will create a plan with a time management system that works for her. (The sooner the better!)

P.S. If they don't want to make a schedule or plan their week, try another suggestion. Ask them to take a few minutes at night to make a list of how they spent their day. Writing down the things they spend their time on can make them aware of how much time they use up getting to classes, in between classes, eating, at meetings, working out, studying, at their job, or what they let slip by on social media and videos or games. That can open some eyes. Everything has to balance. Tell them to plan some fun time, but have them put a limit on it to make the rest of their obligations work. Another Life Lesson. Simple to say, but it may be harder than it sounds.

What can you do?

Prayers for Today

Pray for wise commitments and choices in your son's schedule.

Pray that your daughter learns a system to organize her day that fits her preferences and needs.

Pray for your son to value time for sleep as a non-negotiable element of his schedule.

Pray for chances to redirect their perspective on things that take up their day and pull them back onto a schedule, with comments like, "Are you already done with what you need to do or is this helping somehow?"

What else will you pray for?

21 Why Do They Think That?

Consider this: Five people stood outside of a burning building, trying to deal with what they witnessed. One man pushed against the barricade saying, "What a disaster! I own this building! All my life's savings went toward buying it. If it burns, I will be ruined!"

A woman stood nearby saying, "What a petty thing to be worrying about now. Yes, this is a disaster. My grandmother lives there. What if she didn't get out? I have to find her!"

The next man stood shaking his head and saying, "What's important to me is my son. He's a fireman fighting that inferno. He's still inside. What if he gets burned, or worse?"

Another man pleaded, "My life is over if my studio burns up. I have to get my artwork out. Everything I have ever created is in there. It's a part of me. What if I have nothing left?"

An old woman stood watching with a tear in her eye. She called out, "Has anyone seen my dog? He ran away through the smoke when we rushed out. I'm all alone in this world. He's the only thing I have left to love. What will I do without him?"

People react to things that happen based on their priorities and their personal frame of reference. What matters to one individual, or one college student, may seem trivial to another. What this person hardly notices may create complete heartache for someone else. What matters to you can differ widely from what matters to your son. Your ranking of critical things to accomplish may not have any similarities to your daughter's Must-Do list.

Your son can't live life from your perspective. He needs to evaluate experiences and choose priorities based on his Inner Construct, which he built from the things you taught him combined with the things he experienced and all the emotions he felt along the way. For college students, it's still under development, a work in progress. As they take on more independence and responsibility, they move toward establishing their identities as emerging adults. Each student brings their own different Construct to the table, and that's what creates all these unique individuals with their own perspectives, preferences, and ideas.

People who come into your student's life, like roommates or new boyfriends and girlfriends, may manipulate an Inner Construct. Others introduce political ideals, social conformity, apathy, or even group pressures. Influences from teams or fraternities and sororities undermine their different perspectives and make their newly found footing less sure. Opinions will pile up against your daughter's viewpoints. They may sway her and make her see the world a little differently than the way you see it. Your son may begin to think something you cherish has no value to him. He may find a new driving force for his life which you never gave any value in yours.

Your son may walk up to that burning building and think something completely different from the five people already standing there. Since he does not know anyone who lives there his main concern might be, "What a disaster for the environment. This is a toxic waste dump now. For months I'll be breathing the chemicals these rugs released and the residue from the paint that burned. My girlfriend's asthma was already bad; now with all those irritants in the air she won't be able to breathe." Those ideas did not even come up on your radar when you heard about it. In this situation, no one is considering anyone else, but they are each critical needs from their own point of view. They have different priorities. It's a matter of perspective.

What can you do?

Prayers for Today

Pray that the impending perspective changes your son makes will develop from reputable information and wise influences.

Pray that your daughter will respect family priorities even if her personal priorities shift.

Pray for less attraction to agendas and more development of individual thought.

Pray for understanding and tolerance when ideas clash among family members.

Pray for continued growth, setting good foundation blocks for new ideas and incorporating valid information into strong convictions.

What else will you pray for?

22 Who's Lonely Now?

Your child grew up in your home for most of the last 18 years. You all operated as a family unit, with intertwined needs. Your schedule made accommodations for hers. Your priorities shifted as his preferences developed. One family member's needs swayed decisions this time; another family member had needs met the next time. Family decisions took precedence over personal choices. That pattern helped the overall functioning of the group.

Things have changed now. Mom, you have eliminated quite a lot from your schedule. School programs, sports practices, rehearsals, group project meetings, youth group nights, and a variety of transportation obligations have disappeared from your weekly agenda. In many cases, the transition from high school mom to college mom opens up free time and eliminates commitments (unless a younger child fills those gaps right away). When the changes hit, many moms celebrate their newly found freedom. This often lasts for about two weeks. Then the reality sets in.

You may find yourself lost in a sea of no commitments. You eliminated the obligations that structured your days, so you do not know where to turn. Even moms who still fill their days with other children and full time jobs can face an unexpected challenge to their parental identity. You feel the loss of responsibility for your child, and you miss your involvement in that child's life. We do our best to make them self-sufficient and independent as teens, grooming them for their big step of going off to college. Yet when they do, they take a piece of us along with them. Our kids leave, and they leave behind a hole in our lives and lifestyles. It takes time to find the missing pieces to make new things fit and plug up that hole.

The college transition leaves a lot of moms feeling lonely. It also leaves their kids feeling lonely, even with new roommates and the other 20,000 people on campus. Instead of knowing hundreds of people at their high school, or being able to recognize every face they pass in the halls, they may not see a friend's face for hours on end. Walking around campus, they get lost in a sea of unidentified people as one of the crowd. They may not know a single person in their oversized lecture classes. No one calls out their name or runs up to walk alongside them. They have not dealt with this lack of established identity since starting high school four years ago. They may not even remember the feeling if they transitioned to high school with a large group of friends from middle school.

They will find new friends. They will join new groups and try new activities. If they make the effort to meet people, they will have opportunities to make new friends every day. They will find out how comforting it feels to know that someone knows their name. Your daughter wants to share life with some new friends at college. Your son wants to establish a "bro zone" of friends who will want to experience more of what college life has to offer. Encourage your daughter to move past her discomfort or loneliness and open up to new people. Plenty of other college students want to make new friends now, too. It takes time, but they can find lots of opportunities to meet new people and fill up their social time.

Now step back and focus on you for a moment. You can take charge of how things will go during the next few weeks and months. Will you face your days despondent and lonely, now that your college student has gone away, unhappily saying, "What's next?" Or will you enjoy moving on to your next adventure and say with smiling anticipation, "What's next!?!" Do something for you! You have plenty of choices available to fill your free time now. Think about what you've been putting off for the past few years because you were busy with "mom details." Call up some old friends and catch up on their lives, and see if they're willing to get together. You might feel better about your own feelings when you know it's not just you. Open up to doing something different and trying new things, too, if someone mentions a plan that interests you. Whatever you decide to do, enjoy your time, and share how things are going with your friends and your college student. They will probably enjoy your adventure stories, and they will want to hear more of them as you try new things! You might find that it encourages them to go and do more, too.

What can you do?

Prayers for Today

Pray for your perspective to change as you find new freedom from obligations and move to enjoying your free time.

Pray for the willingness to go after things you have put aside and make your own desires your priority for a change.

Pray for awareness of opportunities to be with people and share their time and their stories.

Pray for other people's willingness to deepen their friendships.

Pray for your son's balance of individual time and group events as he makes new friends.

Pray for the steps your daughter will take to reinforce new friendships so they do not remain superficial acquaintances.

What else will you pray for?

P.S. You can always share stories of how you're managing your new free time at www.lifeasacollegemom101.wordpress.com. I want to read them and hear your ideas!

23 The Choice Is Yours

Colleges operate in perpetual planning motion. The seniors may be graduating, but incoming freshmen have already been welcomed onto campus to take their places. Universities think long term. They post proposed academic calendars for five years, or longer, into the future. Athletic departments plan seasons around potential conference championships, thinking through every step they need to attain months in advance. Housing and Residential Life departments start matching roommates to open dorm rooms about seven months before move-in for the next year. Academic departments plan degree requirements which specify certain courses and sequences needed for completing a major over four years. Things always look ahead, in different timeframes and cycles. There's a lot of planning going on at that campus.

Except in your son's dorm room. He knows he has a meeting with his academic advisor about his course choices for next year. That meeting is soon, as in today at 2:00. But he still does not know what he wants to take. Too many choices to look through. Not enough good class times to take the things he has to take. Not even sure what he has to take.

More gray hairs sprouting? Take a step back, mom. Breathe.

Class scheduling comes around every semester. Some colleges match students with advisors and require two or three planning meetings before choosing schedules. On other campuses, your daughter is on her own to plan her new classes. Forcing students to meet with advisors does not mean the advisor will set their course schedule for them. Many students walk out with a narrowed list, but they are nowhere near their final schedule choices. If they have recently changed majors or have become interested in a new field, they may find they have more choices now than they can process.

The concepts are simple enough: college students need to take classes, so pick some classes that you need to graduate, take them, and graduate. Lots of things get in the way of that straightforward approach. Start with prerequisites, where your son needs to complete some course or evaluation before he can take this course. Some of them back up to the high school level, such as taking a pre-college physics course before you arrive as a freshman in order to take Basics of Engineering. Others depend on performance on placement tests, in foreign languages or for sciences. If your daughter cannot score high enough on a competency test, she can't sign up for Spanish 2, even with four years of high school Spanish under her belt.

Then things get more complicated when your son tries to pick courses. Finding two or three that don't conflict can be easy, but try adding two more, and that will almost guarantee he will hit a time conflict. Some classes only meet in two time slots; if your son already has classes planned for those times, he can't take the additional one he wants. So the disappointment starts. Then he may find that in order to add a different class, he has to take a section with a difficult professor, or even the dreaded unassigned "Staff" instructor.

As soon as your daughter settles on an adequate schedule, she can start the wait-and-see. She logs in to register at her assigned time, but finds that two of the classes she wanted are already full. So, she's back to square one. With each minute that passes, more students register and more classes fill up. Now she has to act fast and pull out her backup plan (or two or three alternates). Then she can plug in a few alternative options and won't lose too much time or too many opportunities. If only she were an honors student or an athlete with priority scheduling…!

My two daughters at two different colleges had very different experiences scheduling for fall semester one year. One daughter had a general idea of which courses she needed and which time slots were available. When she plugged her class choices into the computer during her registration window, she created a near-ideal schedule on her first attempt. No classes before 10am, large windows of open time two days a week for her lab research project, all the best professors, and even Friday afternoons free. What a dream!

My other daughter started planning her schedule with two trips to advisors and a review of what she needed to complete her major. She selected preferred classes and a handful of alternates so she could make quick decisions if she hit a roadblock. She tried to register and quickly realized that most of her options had already closed and now had waiting lists. After several attempts, she settled for seats in two alternate choices and four waiting list spots. Nothing changed to solidify her schedule during the rest of open registration. After closing registration, her college freezes all schedules throughout the summer, making everyone wait to make changes till the "ADD/DROP/SWAP" period before the semester starts. The moment that window opens, computer servers overload and people scramble to take their best shot at working out another schedule. It's more stressful than Black Friday Bargain Shopping!

Thankfully, ADD/DROP/SWAP worked out with a few more openings. These still were not her first choices, but she was satisfied that she would have okay classes. She decided to attend all her waiting list classes the first week while she waited for other peoples' scheduling changes to settle down. She watched her spots on the waiting lists go higher. She wound up getting into one of her more preferred classes and switched another class to a different section to make a better lab time slot work. It all worked out for her.

So, two schedules, two wins, right? Nope. Back to the first daughter, with the perfect schedule. She went to the first day of class and found out that everyone else in the class had taken the professor's elective course prior to this one. Since that was the case, the professor decided to skip all of that information and expected them to review it on their own. It was a necessary part of understanding what they were going to be doing, but since they already knew it, she was not going to spend any class time on it. My daughter asked the professor after class about the material and how much time she needed to spend on learning it. She replied, "Whatever it takes. You need to get up to speed. I usually spend the first four weeks teaching all that. Find a tutor fast."

My daughter decided this setup was too far outside of her comfort zone. She decided to drop that class. When looking to fill the hole in her schedule, she found most of the other classes she would have been happy with were full or conflicted with her existing classes. She decided she could drop another class to fit in a section of a new class, and shift another one into a different time slot. But that conflicted with her lab discussion section. So, she hit the delete button on another class. When all the dust finally settled after a few more moves, she had changed all but one class on her original perfect schedule lineup. Now she had early classes and late evening classes, Friday afternoon lab, and she settled for an unknown instructor. She managed to get through it all, even though it was nothing like what she planned.

That's just a glimpse into the ins and outs of college scheduling. This process is stressful. It is flawed and unfair in ways. The frustration from doing it can send your son running in the opposite direction to avoid the tension. But he has to do it. Please stop yourself if you feel the need to plan it all for him and work out every detail. That may help in the short term, but that does not help him grow. He needs to make decisions about his future which set out steps for him to take. Your daughter has to face the disappointment of having her perfect plan disappear and then pick up the pieces to put together alternatives and keep moving forward. These are life lessons, and they are good ones to learn.

What can you do?

Prayers for Today

Pray for a plan and a path.

Pray for great advice from older students and professors as your daughter evaluates her options.

Pray for your son's resilience to bounce back when choices disappear.

Pray for the planning process so that the better instructors for your daughter will have accessible times.

Pray for good matches with unknown instructors.

Pray for your son's efforts to create a schedule and a long-term plan for his college requirements, that he grows throughout the process and keeps relying on good advice along the way.

What else will you pray for?

24 Is College Worth What It Costs?

When the costs add up and you find yourself asking if it's all really worth it, don't make a quick decision. Money issues during the undergraduate years take a toll on everyone. You watch thousands of dollars going out every month, followed by hundreds for this unplanned extra expense and hundreds more for that surprise. You are not alone if you want to pull the plug on that savings-sucking vacuum.

Feeling the sting of college expenses puts some parents on edge. They want justification from their son for every charge. They follow every autopay notice with a stern conversation about how much it costs for his education. The sticker shock hits hard enough; then every month new charges get added to the bursar bill. If parents did not overestimate their expected financial contributions, their loans or tuition payment plans can fall short by midyear. With all the fees and charges that get included in cost calculators, parents assume everything imaginable has been covered. Wrong! The expenses just keep accumulating.

With that in mind, parents may need to take a step back sometime and make a thorough evaluation of the cost of college compared to their student's performance. Maybe your daughter has struggled in most of her classes and falls far below the required grade point for courses in her major. Your son may have lost interest in his studies, failing to attend class or complete his required assignments. Your daughter may find class boring, and she may start spending a lot of money on more appealing activities or entertainment. That can put an unnecessary burden on your family. Maybe your son chose to drop classes because of poor grades, not realizing you must still pay 75% of the tuition on those classes. He also may not consider that you must pay for them a second time because they are degree requirements which he must re-take. He may also jeopardize his entire Financial Aid package if he falls below a minimum number of credit hours each semester. It keeps adding up. When the cost of having your student continue far outweighs their performance or projected achievement, some serious decisions need to be made.

Facts are facts: some students who start college don't finish college. Some start in one place and transfer to another, for a wide variety of reasons. Some lose direction as they change their mind about a future career. They will need time to re-evaluate what they want from life before starting over in another field. We ask a lot from our 18-year-olds when we expect them to choose a career and an education path before they have even stepped onto a college campus. They haven't experienced much of the world yet and don't know much about the options out there.

Some parents push their students to go after the hardest potential career to get into, like engineering, knowing that many opportunity doors will close once the initial selection process ends. A growing number of colleges now lock admission to selective programs, informing any interested students that they must be accepted into them as incoming freshmen. They do not allow any transfers into the program later. That means if there's any chance your daughter wants an engineering degree there, she has to be accepted into it when she chooses that school. All these elements add up to students choosing to follow paths they're not committed to. It sets them up for chaos when they change their direction and need to re-invent themselves later. They will need a new identity and a new plan as a student in another major.

If your son cannot picture himself taking a job in the field he is studying, it's clearly time for a change. That change may come as an easy decision with a new plan, or it might involve a long process of serious doubt and wayward wandering. When he makes a simple switch of paths, it is easier to encourage him to adjust and continue, making up for lost time where he can. When the plan loses focus and your daughter can't decide if she should become a teacher, or an accountant, or maybe even a dentist, she may be better off taking some time away from school to determine a direction instead of stopping and starting such unrelated options. Encourage her to find out how her college gives credit for classwork completed outside of the major. At some schools, it counts toward core requirements across college divisions and has an impact on graduation. At others, its value is only the lessons learned against the price you paid for the courses, and that means your daughter will be starting over with no applicable credits. Take a good look at what another choice will mean before you support your student's decision.

What can you do?

Prayers for Today

Pray for your daughter's career choice, that it reflects her true calling and her desires in life.

Pray for awareness of your son's indecision, before he gets frustrated or loses hope.

Pray for perseverance through challenging coursework so that your daughter does not abandon a dream at the first sign of difficulty.

Pray for your son to think through related options before completely changing direction.

Pray for strong advisors and exposure to useful experiences which will help guide your student in making choices.

Pray for patience and endurance if your daughter decides to change her plans completely or leave school until she makes another career choice.

What else will you pray for?

25 Accidents Happen

I heard that two very different things lead this year's list of items most often involved in on-campus injuries. Any guesses?

Two completely unrelated diabolical menaces: bunk beds and rented power scooters.

As a mom, you hear something like that and you cringe a little. You spent years teaching your son every safety lesson you knew about dangerous items like box cutters and drain cleaner. You covered not overloading the power strip and taping down loose throw rugs. You felt that Life Lessons in other areas would create a blanket of protection for odd occurrences which might put your daughter at risk. You gave your son swimming lessons, first aid classes, and sent him for a week of survival skills training to prepare for life away from home.

And now, you find out the most common threats to his safety involve falling off a scooter (a powered skateboard with a handle) or falling out of bed.

Instead of rushing off to write an email strictly forbidding any contact with these two hazards, maybe you can start a conversation about things that happen unexpectedly. Tell your son you just heard that fact, and ask him if he knows anyone who has been injured by those two culprits. He may have some interesting stories to share, like this one a mom told me:

> "Mom, Kellie hyper-extended her knee and now she's on crutches," my daughter told me.
>
> "I didn't know she was an athlete. What does she play?"
>
> "She's not in any sports, Mom."

"Did she fall?" I asked.

"No. Well, not really. She missed the last step when she was getting out of her bunk bed and her leg bent backward when she hit the floor."

"Ouch! That hurts just thinking about it. How long will she be on crutches?" I winced at the thought.

"Four weeks. If she tore a ligament, she might need surgery."

My concern is real. "So, does this make you want to change your bed from a lofted one back down to the floor now? Please?"

I can see it in the headlines: "College co-ed taken out by a lofted bed... and not even from falling off." Unbelievable!

Moms get lectured about worrying too much all the time. Well, it's hard not to worry when you hear stories like that. Instead, offer a reminder about a potential hazard that bothers you, and then have faith that your daughter will do her best to stay safe. If your son has become a frequent rider of rental scooters and uses them every day, remind him to look out for unsuspecting people stepping into his path. Tell him to keep an eye out for shuttles and campus vehicles on less-traveled side roads. Lots of visitors to college campuses don't interact with scooters in their everyday lives. They do not realize the dangers of having riders share their paths. Reminders can seem like nagging, but they can bring up things which your son never even considers as he uses the scooter.

When someone else's accidents happen, your college student may feel the impact as an innocent victim. Falling off a scooter will hurt one person; if riders run into nearby people while they crash it causes multiple injuries. There have even been reports of hit-and-runs, where a scooter rider hits a pedestrian and doesn't stop to help or take responsibility. Bunk beds can be the site of accidents caused by someone else, too, when a person jokingly pushes another person off a bed and they fall hard. A few feet off the ground and a bad landing can mean a sprain or a broken bone, or even a long-term back injury. Not a happy thought, but something to try to get them to think about.

Carelessness causes a majority of accidents on campus and throughout the rest of the world. By pointing out some ways to stay aware of safety and consideration of others, you're building a better future for all of us.

What can you do?

Prayers for Today

Pray for the college years to go by without any major accidents.

Pray for your son's safety interacting with other students on campus.

Pray for attentive care if an accident occurs.

Pray for your daughter's awareness of her surroundings to avoid any dangers on campus.

Pray for all campus travelers to be more aware of people and vehicles around them.

Pray for people to follow safety rules while living in the dorms and not be a danger to others in the building.

Pray for quick discovery of dangers and for actions to remove them.

What else will you pray for?

26 Mistaken Identity

One college student's mom sent me a picture of a laundry room in his dorm. A pile of folded clothes sat on top of a dryer with this note:

> To whoever owns these clothes:
>
> Your MIA clothes have returned after seven fun-filled days in Chicago with me. Because I was rushing to catch the airport shuttle before break, I grabbed my laundry out of my dryer and stuffed it into my suitcase. When I got there, I realized that I didn't have my own clothes. I hope your break went better than mine. I also hope you know where my clothes are now, since you obviously moved them when you put yours into the dryer I was using. Can you please leave them here for me?

You probably didn't cover hunting for lost stuff in your college preparation talks.

> Another mom told me her son's story of moving around desks to work in groups during one Thursday afternoon class, leaving everyone's belongings sitting in piles around the room. At the end of the class, someone else picked up his laptop and walked out. He looked for it, but by the time he realized it was missing, most of the other students and the professor had left. The laptop that remained unclaimed was an exact copy of his, but it was password protected and did not have a name on it, so he could not find out who owned it. He contacted the professor and received her email late Friday afternoon saying she would email the rest of the class to find the owner. The other student didn't read the email until Sunday and had no idea he had picked up the wrong laptop, so he ignored it. The next class met the following Tuesday. Only after the professor opened the laptop at the front of the room and

showed the locked screen did the original owner realize it was his. Then he had to make arrangements to meet to give back the wrong computer later because he had not brought it with him to class.

It was a case of mistaken identity. "No harm intended," but plenty occurred. He had no idea what trouble he caused by picking up the wrong laptop. The real owner had everything else he needed for his other classes on that computer and was stonewalled for five days without his notes and files.

People make mistakes. In our world of mass-produced and brand-labeled goods, you probably have looked at something familiar and questioned, "Is that mine?" Think about how often you see a phone left behind on a table. If it did not have a unique cover to show it was obviously someone else's, every person walking by would pick it up and turn it on to see if it was theirs.

If things are not tied to owners on leashes, the chance exists that they will vanish. Whether we lose them or someone else takes them, they can disappear. We hope they are just missing, and that your student can backtrack and find them again. That is a bit of a challenge, after walking 20,000 steps across campus during the day. It is also frustrating, since some facilities collect lost items at a central location, while others leave things right where people left them in the hopes the owner will return to claim them. Some campuses have piles of jackets, textbooks, backpacks, calculators, lab goggles, and sports gear sitting in lost-and-found departments. Your son may leave things at places ranging from the cafeteria, to a bench outside a classroom, or even on a campus bus. Your daughter may walk away from a tote bag on the side of a desk, or leave her flash drive in a shared printer terminal. They cover a lot of miles in a day, so their things could be anywhere.

Even if things do not turn up right away, there is still a chance that your son will find his missing items. Encourage him to go back to everywhere he has already looked and ask again a few weeks later. People have been known to return things they mistook for their own when they finally realize they have the wrong thing. After items sit unclaimed for a while, they might get sent on to a central lost property location. If your daughter keeps trying, she may find her missing items among the piles of other lost stuff one day. That will be a good day!

What can you do?

Prayers for Today

Pray for quick recovery of missing items.

Pray for your daughter's awareness as she leaves a place that she has what she needs and she takes what she brought with her.

Pray for your son to take responsibility for his things when he goes places on campus.

Pray for gentle nudges and realization that things are being left behind before your student leaves the area.

Pray for honesty and integrity of people who come across lost items to turn them in instead of taking them.

Pray that important things stay safely in your daughter's hands.

Pray for your son to help others recover their missing items by turning in things he finds instead of leaving them behind.

What else will you pray for?

27 It's All Greek To Me

Greek life on campus can take many forms. Some affiliations with fraternities and sororities involve little more than paying a yearly fee and attending a few meetings. Other groups expect every member to be an active participant in every event they have on campus, as well as to live and eat with fellow members in a chapter house. Some Greeks establish lifelong friendships with their brothers or sisters after experiencing college life together. Others feel their experiences were not worth the effort, after years of submission to chapter rules and unrealistic expectations. The expectations do not always match the experiences. Even within the fraternal bond of brotherhood or sisterhood, individual members can find they have different social acceptance and status among their fellow members. Just like in any family, not all the brothers and sisters get along... or even like each other.

Pledging takes time, money, and effort, and does not guarantee an acceptance into the group. After enduring weeks of submissive evaluations, your son may find he does not get offered a place alongside the few selected recruits. Your daughter may receive an invitation to join her chosen chapter, but faces a dilemma when her closest friends get passed by. On most campuses, joining a Greek community includes accepting that the chapter now takes the most important social role in your student's life. All other friendships and associations, no matter how important they once were, become lower priorities for your son's time and involvement.

Greek life offers a built-in network of friends. It fills a calendar with time commitments. In recent years, Greek life obligations have spilled over into travel weekends and trip plans for semester breaks and vacations (usually with an added cost, even if they are mandatory). Advance planning for activities may bring your daughter to campus before the semester starts, or keep her there during holidays. National affiliates may require attendance at regional meetings or conventions. Projects and charity efforts can take hours of planning and managing, and involve extra expenses to take part. Add that to the thousands of dollars most Greeks charge their chapter members every year, and the totals can astound you.

Greek life can offer plenty in return for the time and the expense. Friendships abound. Living with responsibilities and obligations will develop your daughter's managerial capabilities. Learning to live with a variety of people in a shared space moves your son along to a new level of maturity. Having a bond with people who share a common identity makes facing college life difficulties a little easier. Looking long term, developing friendships and connections which your son can rely on for the rest of his life can help him throughout his future and his career, even after moving to another area of the country.

While most campus Greek communities accommodate a member's outside commitments, some Greek chapters avoid accepting students on sports teams. They feel their members should take on the identity of their fraternity, not of a team. They want full participation at scheduled events, and that often conflicts with games and practices. If your daughter wants to play volleyball and has too many time conflicts, she may be rejected during rush week. Knowing this little-publicized fact can save her the heartache and disappointment from not being accepted.

Another downside of Greek communities involves their promotion of drinking, parties, and at-risk behaviors. If your student has trouble standing her ground, she may feel overpowered by the crowd mentality within the chapter. When your son decides he has had enough, the chanting crowd might convince him to have even more. In a normal campus interaction, he could simply walk away, but this involves jeopardizing all his community and identity connections.

Every year, thousands of college students across the country wait with anticipation for the start of Greek Week. Let's hope each one matches with a good group to build lifelong friendships and develop a new element of their identity.

What can you do?

Prayers for Today

Pray for complete awareness in making a decision to pursue Greek life.

Pray for the compatibility of your son and his fraternity brothers. Pray for the development of lifelong friendships.

Pray that your daughter will fully understand her commitment to the chapter and its activities before she joins.

Pray for your son's ability to balance his studies and his fraternity life.

Pray that your daughter will adjust to having time commitments to her sorority.

Pray for the safety of all students in the Greek system and for maturity and respect when dealing with each other.

What else will you pray for?

28 We Just Can't Go On Like This Anymore

When two roommates can't get along, everything suffers. A "perfect roommate" does not exist on this side of heaven, partly because of the different desires each person has in their arrangement. Plenty of reasonable expectations exist in the world of dorm room sharing; the problem comes in getting two roommates to think about what the other person wants and to make their preferences work together. Without some compromises and understanding, all roommates can plan on hitting some rough patches.

A large part of the College Life experience includes sharing space and time with another human being. Whether your son hand-picked his future roommate out of hundreds of pages of Roommate Search profiles, or your daughter took a blind match by the Residence Life staff, the process has major pitfalls. Neither way provides a failsafe assurance that the two people share enough compatibility to make it work.

Too many college moms can share stories of what happens when roommates do not get along. Some students decide to stick it out, even if it means living with the cold shoulder or having a maximum of three words spoken in their presence in a given day. Your son may feel that his other friendships more than compensate for the lack of a relationship with his roommate, so he will put up with it for the rest of the semester. Or, your daughter may decide the tension and lack of consideration drives her crazy, and she needs to get out of their shared space as soon as possible.

When the first big blow-up occurs, ask about the details to understand what happened. Often you will hear only one side of a complicated exchange. Without knowing her roommate's side of the story, you risk giving your daughter unmerited sympathy or bad advice. Remember: you didn't witness it, and the version you hear has a definite bias to it. Thankfully, your distance from the confrontation, and your own life experience, may give you a better perspective on the conflict than your wounded daughter has. Your son may have chosen to stand firm for an ideal when the relationship could improve with a compromise. Whatever the case, looking past the argument and on toward a resolution makes the most sense. Getting your son to understand that, though, may not be an easy task.

In the end, any major conflict will finish with one of two results: the roommates decide to remain roommates or decide to move on. Your daughter needs support, even if you don't agree with her ultimate decision or with the way she handled things along the way. Your son may face a mountain of difficulty in finding a new roommate, moving his belongings, and establishing a new roommate relationship. After it, he will remember the conflict he just lived through, and will take a better approach to sharing a room with the next person. Encourage your daughter to talk about the things that went wrong in dealing with her ex-roommate, so the new arrangements can be better from the start. The conflict that brought your son to this point has pushed him a little further along in his progress toward adulthood. It may sting, it may bruise, it may topple over a lofty tower, but in the aftermath, your daughter will realize she has stepped a little farther down the path to maturity. Getting through conflicts can show her what she's made of, and what she's ready to handle in life. Another Life Lesson learned.

What can you do?

Prayers for Today

Pray for a balance between standing up for something and working toward a resolution of conflict.

Pray for extra awareness and consideration on both roommates' parts.

Pray for reasonable dialogue about preferences and needs when one roommate feels the other has overstepped the limits.

Pray for quieted tempers and kind words as arguments develop.

Pray for your daughter's patience with having another human in her space.

Pray for your son's habits, in learning to maintain the expected level of respect for his roommate as he manages the responsibilities of living away from home.

What else will you pray for?

Check-In Time

Have your prayers for your college student changed since you started reading this book? Which topic made the biggest impact so far? What Life Lessons did your student learn on their own? Which ones had you missed in your preparations? Share a little of your story with me and other moms by commenting at:
www.lifeasacollegemom101.wordpress.com

And keep praying!

29 That's Not What I Meant

Our world has changed. People used to have fewer opportunities to share their opinions with anyone but their friends and work associates. An occasional Letter to the Editor or appearance at a town council meeting might have given you the opportunity to speak your mind. In today's over-connected society, every time someone has an opinion or idea, they feel obligated to share it with their 2,496 followers on Twitter and another 1,863 of their Instagram friends. Do you hate being swamped with useless messages debating current brew choices each time someone shows up at a local coffee shop? You will not drop what you are doing and go meet them there. (Although, it might be fun to show up and say you took that as an invitation to join them. And, of course, that means they're paying, right?!)

But beyond all the "Look at me, I'm here" posts and family photos, these social platforms also give everyone the chance to speak their mind as often as they want. Politics, relationships, likes and dislikes, and controversial topics abound in post after post on your son's feed. Readers confuse opinions with facts, since nothing comes from a reliable source anymore. Things that sound good get shared and re-shared without any chance to verify information, and conflicting views or questions get deleted quickly.

For generations, college campuses have encouraged individual thinking, as places for progressive ideas and open exchanges. Collegiate debates have changed now. Access to the internet has changed the "speaking up" process from a few students defending their strongly held beliefs to people always sharing their minds about their reactions to something they heard or read. Plenty of internet users do not realize the distinction between platforming and posting an opinion. Your son may have spent the last five years "liking" posts and reacting to things his friends said. He may lack actual knowledge about anything he comments on. But to another person reading his posts, he sounds like an expert. Your daughter will find that hundreds of people will like a comment she makes sharing facts about the environment, even if she has just made it all up!

If your son enjoys getting confirmation of his opinions, the internet can become a dangerous place. Scoring a handful of likes will encourage him to post something else, and that leads to more likes and followers. Having followers is worthless unless you keep telling them what you have to say, so that means more time spent on more posts. Getting people to react takes a little controversy, so next he will throw that in. And soon you are reading post after post supporting some radical thought which could get him kicked off campus. (This is not a fairy tale — it really happens.) When you talk to him and ask about why he feels so strongly about this controversy, you may hear, "What? That's not what I meant."

Some of our daughters and sons enter college without ever having cared about important topics before. They've never developed an informed opinion and have never faced challenges to think about where they stand on an issue. Back in high school, classmates who cared about controversial things were seen as eccentrics, wasting their time on things that didn't matter. Now starting college, they move onto campus and meet scores of people with critical agendas who expect their support.

Sometimes the fact that a friend has joined a cause will propel your daughter to enlist, too. A noble speech by a student on a bench on the quad can drive your son to start promoting a group and its events. He and his friends may need the reminder to find out what they're supporting, especially if an outside organization backs the effort. Even if working for this goal sounds right, if the group's core principles support completely different views than your daughter holds, she may need to back away from it. She may find that students who participate in the activity get labeled by other people on campus as "supporters" or "one of them." That can be hard to dispute or disprove, even if it is not what she believes.

What can you do?

Prayers for Today

Pray for maturity as your son decides where and when to speak his mind.

Pray for ongoing dialogue between your daughter and any friends who hold different opinions than hers.

Pray for transparency of each organization's agendas, before a firm commitment to participate takes place.

Pray for wisdom as your son decides which stands he will take.

Pray for clear messages by speakers across campus, so their truth, and not their appeal, draws people in.

Pray for self-set limits to reactions and opinions when your daughter interacts with friends on social media, to prevent her from saying what she does not mean to say.

What else will you pray for?

30 Growing Up a Little Too Fast

Relationships move college students into a new phase of reality. Each person your son interacts with will impact his personality. We expect and appreciate some changes, as he matures and takes on more responsibility. Other transformations seem like disappointing consequences, absorbed from unwise influences. Changes involve choices, and even if your daughter is unprepared for them, here they come. Mom, your prayers may need to kick into overdrive sooner than you ever imagined.

College life is packed full of choices: roommates, classes, where to live, what to eat, groups to join. These matter in their everyday lives. Some things matter more, though, and have a bigger impact on life. Picking up habits, developing a lifestyle, or getting into a long-term relationship have stronger influences on any college student's future. Moms can pray and complain and worry and pray some more, and still feel their student's life will spin out of control based on the choices they have made.

Plenty of people have made it through life after making choices which their parents hated. Their decisions may have destroyed plans, compromised trust, and shattered family values. In their eyes, parents' expectations come from an outdated perspective which has no relevance in their new world. But, to their parents, the concepts of disappointment, disrespect, and disobedience could all apply.

Choices are personal selections, and as students make decisions, they set their futures in motion. Sorry that this might make you uncomfortable, but we need to bring up the serious legal and moral stuff now. Underage alcohol use usually comes up first, since it is so prevalent on campuses. Watching others will influence how appealing drinking and partying are to your student. With the legalization of marijuana in 12 states, that's another choice they'll be facing. Add in the exposure to other drug or stimulant use. Then add on premarital sex and moving in together. Some may consider leaving their religion. Now you have the top five life choices they will face. There are plenty more. Each of these serious decisions involves consequences, too. You may come to terms with your daughter moving in with her boyfriend, but you may face an entirely new challenge if she finds out she's pregnant.

If they grow up a little too fast, they may find a lot of their choices collide with their hopes and dreams for the future. If your son gets caught with recreational drugs and gets a criminal record, the opportunity for him to become a high school teacher as he planned may disappear. If your daughter has a child, her responsibilities will change and impact the options she can consider. Beyond pregnancy, the physical consequences of having sex are very real and can impact both partners. Lifelong conditions like herpes and HPV have negative effects which your unsuspecting 19- or 20-year-old isn't considering.

With so many outside influences telling them how to enjoy life, college students face some tough choices. Abandoning what they believed till now can seem like the only option when their new preferences collide with established family values. Instead of working through their beliefs and defending their thoughts, they take drastic steps to detach from the past and start an independent life.

As a parent, you may be blindsided and find little hope in reconnecting on common ground. Throughout it all, try to remember that you are dealing with an emerging adult who has made personal choices. That right belongs to them, even if you disagree with their decisions. You raised them to take on life; now step back and watch as they do it.

What can you do?

Prayers for Today

Pray that your son's moral convictions stay strong through his exposure to new challenges at college.

Pray that they will make the right decisions on small choices along the way which impact big future life choices.

Pray for uplifting relationships which offer companionship with friends who share your daughter's beliefs.

Pray for the strength to face the conflict that comes with choices.

Pray that your son's friends will not overwhelm his concept of right and wrong with their lifestyle choices.

Pray for your daughter's ability to respect your beliefs even if hers have changed.

What else will you pray for?

31 Cards and Care Packages

A friend told me this story: My daughter's friend never gave her school address to anyone when she left for college. She rarely received mail at home and had no reason to expect that anyone would send her anything. She went weeks at a time without opening her mailbox, assuming if anything at all showed up, it would be junk mail.

After a while, she began to get a little jealous of my daughter. My freshman was a postal superstar, and a day without mail was a rarity. She had a constant flow of cards, letters, care packages, postcards, and an occasional catalog or sale flyer. You see, before she left for school, she sent an email with her new mailing address and email to everyone she knew, asking people to keep in touch. Kids she babysat sent crayon drawings for all the holidays. Her friends from other schools sent postcards saying, "Wish you were here!" Relatives sent candy bars and hot cocoa. Her grandmother sent her cards in envelopes covered with silly stickers. Grandma also signed her up for free trial issues of six or seven new magazines during the first semester (even though her granddaughter didn't have the time to read most of them).

None of those items was a cherished gift. Nothing was extremely valuable or memorable. But it's the thought that counts. She loved knowing that people were thinking of her and that they were taking a little time out of their day to share their lives with her. My daughter's friend watched this, and her jealousy grew. She would make sarcastic comments about the mail and find things to criticize about the gifts. She would walk away instead of waiting while my daughter stopped to pick up her mail. It took a while for my daughter to realize what was bothering her friend. She came up with a brilliant solution. She sent her mail! First, she left cards for her under her door. Then my daughter left her a note saying she had a package to pick up (which had a silly drawing and one of her favorite sodas in it). After that, she encouraged her friend to let others know that receiving a little mail would brighten her day. If she didn't ask for a little contact, my daughter told her friend, she wasn't going to get any.

Sometimes the little things mean the most. In our world of electronic communication and artificial intelligence, college students living away from home can feel different kinds of separation from their families and friends. They miss seeing the people they know, especially on large campuses where they are one of thousands. If they come from large families, they miss the interactions in daily life routines. When contact with their friends slows down, they feel they are missing out on their lives, too. A little mail from home can help fill those gaps.

Small shots of encouragement can carry a college student through rough times. When classes pour on the workload and your daughter feels swamped, being reminded of people she cares about can boost her spirits and give her a renewed strength. Feeling cared about by them in return can double the effect.

So, if you can arrange a little mailbox activity, do it! Your daughter might be shocked and delighted to find an unexpected card from a neighbor or a cousin. Your son can keep friendships going with younger members of his teams who stay in touch. Even hearing from a youth group leader that the entire group is praying for her will make her day. It all brings home a bit closer. It makes your student remember that they are remembered. A little contact from the home front can make any day a little brighter.

Here's an idea, mom: Organize a group of 10 or 12 moms to meet for a care package stuffing party. Tell each mom to choose something small that they think their own student would like as a treat (no liquids or perishables) and bring 12 of that thing. Get everyone to pitch in a few dollars to cover postage costs. Assemble 12 packages with one of each treat, add in a card signed by every mom, and ship them off to their campus mailboxes. I can guarantee you will hear from them when they get them. Ask them to take pictures with their care packages to share with all the moms who helped. Here's the real treat: what comes in the box will not be as important as knowing 12 moms care about them.

I would love to hear about your care package parties. Share your ideas for things to include, your love notes, and any fun ways to package it all up. Did you pick a theme, or was everyone creative on their own? Share your stories of what your son or daughter said, too. Did he mention an item that was a real hit? Did she share her gifts with her friends? Let me know how this works for you at: **www.lifeasacollegemom101@wordpress.com**

What can you do?

Prayers for Today

Pray that you will find ways to continually encourage your son, through calls, emails, notes, letters, or packages.

Pray for awareness of things that would be special surprises to lift your daughter out of a bad day.

Pray in appreciation of the efforts of others.

Pray that your son feels gratitude, and he appreciates the effort others have made to stay in contact.

Pray for your daughter's willingness to reach out to others even when their contact has diminished.

Pray for your son's interest in spreading kindness with his own notes and letters to friends and family.

What else will you pray for?

32 Tell Me Anything

A friend and her daughters had an understanding about sensitive topics. She told her daughters early in their teens they could talk to her about anything. They had open, honest discussions about life, with the conversations moving to more serious questions as they grew up. She didn't know what she was in for. When they started to bring up topics that reached far outside her comfort zone, her initial reactions surprised the girls. They needed a safe place to discuss concerns and sensitive issues, and thought their mom would provide it. She was willing, and very capable to offer advice and good counsel. The problem was the shock value.

When her daughters told her about their friends' decisions and difficulties, she had a hard time keeping her emotions out of her reactions. She needed a few moments to deal with her surprise, her disappointment at the choices, or her fears regarding the situations they described. They were natural, honest, motherly reactions… but they were not the ones that her daughters needed at the time. The girls were looking for solid advice and potential solutions, not emotions. But there are some conversations you never want to have, some things you do not want to hear. After a few of these talks ended badly, she decided to have a sideline discussion with them so she could explain her point of view and her reactions without dealing with a crisis at the same time.

Talking about the poor communication helped. She let her daughters know that she cared deeply about the people who needed help and wanted to be ready to help them. My friend asked her daughters to consider starting a sensitive talk with her in a new way. She asked the girls to start by saying bluntly, "Here we go again. No judgments, Mom!"

It was enough of a verbal cue to set her perspective into a non-emotional framework. She could keep a detached viewpoint since she had that clear reminder to think that way. She knew how her mind worked and knew this would work for her. They used that method successfully all through their time at college. The stories kept coming, and she offered advice and direction when asked for it. As time went on, she became more of a sounding board instead of an advice giver. Her daughters started incorporating things they had already learned into crafting their own advice for friends, and then shared how it worked with their mother afterward.

We all wish our college students and their friends could make it through their four years without having major difficulties. Some have things happen to them. Some do things to themselves. Some deal with mental challenges we never knew about. Some struggle with inner scars and instability. When things start falling apart, they may reach out for a lifeline. They probably won't ask more than once or twice, so you only have a brief opportunity to respond. Stay willing to listen, even if it sounds worse than a sensational movie plot. If they bring it up, it matters in their life. If you try to help and fail, try again. If they come back to you, whatever the problem, move past the shock value and offer some suggestions they can consider. You may be their only connection to a rational perspective. It might be hard to hear some details, but if they reach out, they need you. Ready or not, it's coming.

What can you do?

Prayers for Today

Pray for awareness of your own emotional buffer, and for developing skill at using it.

Pray for your ability to reduce the times you need to use that buffer.

Pray for your daughter's skills at listening to friends in their time of need and offering solid advice.

Pray for your son's compassion and recommendation-giving skills to develop.

Pray that your daughter stays attentive for opportunities to reach out to someone who is struggling.

Pray for the established support centers on campus to work effectively to help any students in need.

What else will you pray for?

33 Fragile Children

Every mother carries burdens while raising her children. We take on the caregiving and teaching. We listen to their disappointments. We nurture and guide, while protecting and defending them. We cover them in prayer for the things beyond our reach. We feel their wounds and try to prevent future ones.

We love them, head to toe, and have a natural instinct to help them thrive.

In special cases, our children need extra help. They may have physical or emotional difficulties which have challenged them throughout their lives. Some moms have spent as much time at doctor's offices as others did at playgrounds while their children grew. They know the ins and outs of clinics and urgent care centers. Some have waited patiently during long illnesses for the day their son could be released from the hospital. Others have had to fight their own emotions and stay strong to keep up their daughter's spirits during a long battle. They want to watch them live long and happy lives, and have some valid concerns that they will not get that chance. Getting them to the brink of adulthood has taken courage and determination. Sending these kids off to college takes an entirely different level of mom-power.

Some moms have spent years as a vigilant protector. One family I know lives on constant alert for exposure to food allergens. The smallest contact with nuts or shellfish sends these kids into anaphylactic shock. Over the past ten years they have needed emergency intervention for accidental exposure at least four times that I recall, probably more. Their lives outside the home have always been risky ventures, and they have lived tethered to Epi-pens for years. The high school they attended made accommodations, and they informed other parents of foods to avoid sending in lunches, but it still happened. Soon they will step onto a college campus and face many more unknowns. How does a mom who has been on high alert for the past eighteen years simply step back now and say, "Go ahead. Have a good year!"? She can't. And she shouldn't.

Most of us with fragile children have learned how to ask for accommodations. We play a crucial role in monitoring how well others take on responsibilities for supervising our student's care. Most campus staff welcome this kind of parent involvement: it is not hand-holding and expecting special privileges, it is dealing with legitimate concerns for the wellbeing of one of their students. When your son has survived a life-threatening illness, you do not want to see him face another challenge because he is not allowed to dispense his own medications. You can check on the availability of campus advocates who can help contact professors if your daughter misses classes for treatments. You can meet with the dorm safety director when you realize your mobility-challenged son's only access to his room is by an elevator in the opposite wing of the building. In cases like these, students should still take the lead, but parental involvement as care managers can make things happen.

Whether your student has huge issues or small needs, chronic ones or unexpected flare-ups, your concerns are valid and real. You have been through this enough to know that you are dealing with more than typical care issues. Have some serious conversations with your son about his care and his needs. Explain how you have advocated for him in the past and show him how to advocate for himself. Make sure the right people know about your daughter's condition and can step in if she needs help. Don't let a standard protocol make you uncomfortable about what you and your son agree he needs for his individual care. At some point, though, the time will come to accept that you can only do so much. Advocate, explain, and ask for help. Then you have to let go. And pray.

Your daughter's heart condition, or your son's blood counts, or anything else they deal with, have become a part of their lives. They will continue to face whatever they have been dealing with as they start a new life on campus. There may be setbacks. You may wind up in another care facility after another difficulty. But you are letting them experience life and become an adult. Wasn't that what it was all about in the first place?

What can you do?

Prayers for Today

Pray for special care and protection for your child.

Pray for your son to stay strong and healthy while living on campus.

Pray for caregivers to provide the specific support your daughter needs in managing her condition.

Pray for the other moms who are learning to rely on new people as the front line of support for their sons or daughters.

Pray that if your daughter needs special accommodations, she will get them.

Pray that your son finds supportive friends who understand his challenges and work through them with him.

Pray that no one would face a need for urgent help in dire situations.

Pray for your daughter to have a long, fulfilling life and get beyond the difficulties she faces.

What else will you pray for?

34 Mental Health Days

We all need a break once in a while. College students are no exception. They become slaves to their assignment calendars and extra-curricular obligations. Their days are packed full of classes, activities, jobs, dorm life, and meetings. They try to juggle appointments and review sessions, and they still have to find time to do laundry.

Even with all these commitments, they get disappointed at missing out on things. Someone else gets to go to all the basketball games or see all the free movies. Speakers, plays, and concerts fill performance halls every weekend, but chances are if your daughter gets to one a year, she's giving up something else to go. Her grades depend on her study time and doing work outside of class, which takes up most of the free time in her schedule. But she will squeeze in a few more things this week because she wants to do them. College would not be college without all the things to do!

Smart students realize that all these time-takers take a toll on their minds. Their frenetic pace can only keep going for so long before physical and mental exhaustion kick in. A lot of students think that relaxing means doing things instead of studying. They do not understand that doing something else is still doing something; it is not resting. Brain-engaging efforts like listening to a podcast will keep the neurons firing, when what they really need is a cooldown session. Grabbing a basketball for a pickup game may give your son some needed social interaction and physical exertion, but it might not help. His competitive nature uses high-level cerebral functioning as he calls out plays and strategizes with other team members. His brain may even work harder on the court than when he sits in class.

They need time to de-stress, unwind, disengage, and download. This involves more than just catching up on lost sleep or binge-watching a comedy TV show. It takes the "shut yourself away alone for a few hours to rest your mind" kind of thing. Your son may think that wastes his time, which he doesn't have enough of anyway. Your daughter may feel uncomfortable releasing pent-up stress because it has been fueling her for so long. She will get a renewed energy level and sense of control by taking a step away from her pressures for a change.

Remind your son that by releasing his cares for a while, he can give his mind a chance to rest. We all function better after resting. If recharging relieves some of the tensions clouding your daughter's reasoning, her cleared mind will move through tasks easier. Calming a few frazzled emotions will put her back on a productive path. Your son's renewed body will carry him farther. He will accomplish more after resting than he would if he continued while weighed down with fatigue and concerns.

Taking advantage of quiet time to disengage is like turning off your computer for a hard reboot. You do not even realize how many conflicting programs have slowed your system until you see it zipping along again after it restarts. We all need a hard reboot once in a while. And that means something different for every person. Some decide a quiet room is all they need. Others may try meditation. Some like to incorporate movement, like walking through a park or doing yoga. Encourage your son to try a few different methods when he starts on this journey. Reassure your daughter that if it does not work the first time, it is not a waste of time to try again. It takes a few attempts for our minds to let go. Take your own Mental Health Day once in a while and encourage your student to take one, too.

What can you do?

Prayers for Today

Pray for your son's willingness to take time to recharge.

Pray that your daughter lightens her load and gives herself some breathing room.

Pray for understanding that stepping away for a moment is not the same as avoiding your responsibilities.

Pray that early attempts give encouraging results so your son will continue to search for balance.

Pray for awareness when mental pressures are building and for taking steps to find the right help.

Pray for anyone on campus facing serious mental struggles, that they connect with capable caregivers and willingly accept help.

What else will you pray for?

35 More Choices Ahead

As our college students quickly find out, university life offers more choices than they ever imagined. They may struggle with FOMO (Fear Of Missing Out), packing their daily schedule with all the things they want to do in 24 hours. Having a few options can offer incredible opportunities to students enjoying their newly acquired independence. As they transition through their years on campus, they will find that the future offers them even more choices ahead.

Early decisions for students most often include choosing new roommates and where they will live next year. Sometimes those two come in a package deal, if their new roommates already know where they want to live. Other times they are two very different challenges, taking a lot of work and time. Transitioning to living off campus instead of in dorms may be the next big choice. Your son could pick from a hundred different places. But he needs to consider location, cost, and whether the place meets his needs. He also needs to understand his responsibilities and expenses as a renter. Many housing options open for brief windows as leases expire, and staying aware of the available locations can become its own full-time job during the search.

Another important decision coming soon involves committing to a major. If your son has changed majors along the way, he may have chosen a similar field or something entirely new. At least he selected something, and he is heading toward finishing again. When your daughter tries to plan out her life based on a career, and then changes her mind on the goal, she may hesitate to commit to a new major. Her fear of failing again makes it easier to keep looking at all the options instead of making a new choice. If you step in with a little advice here it might help her. Try to encourage her to investigate her options only for a limited time. At that point, she needs to move ahead with the next best choice based on what she has learned.

When they get those selections under their belts, they can look forward to their job choices. Their selected major should have led them along a career path, narrowing down options to a handful of potential positions When they start looking for actual employment in those fields, they may see the world open up in front of them again. Your daughter may find entirely unexpected jobs which hire graduates with her major. Picking a job to pursue might overwhelm your son, let alone having to decide the city where he wants to live to take a job like that. In some careers, your first few positions set the stage for the employment options you'll be able to consider in the future. For example, most school principals have spent years in direct teaching roles and then have transitioned into managerial roles based on experience and capabilities. In other fields, like communications, jobs offer a wide range of responsibilities and expectations depending on the company and the position. If your daughter has a specific career goal, she needs to find out which job path will take her there.

If your son can handle these important choices, then he will learn to handle all the other choices coming down the line. He will face bigger and more pivotal choices all through life. Your daughter may enjoy having options and become an expert at evaluating opportunities to make a worthwhile selection. When your son finds that an option he preferred has gone away, he may need to regroup before deciding on an alternative path. He may choose something after quickly considering a few options, or he may commit a lot of time and energy into picking something new. Your daughter may approach making choices with hesitancy, asking for your guidance along the way. Or, she may make surprise announcements of things she decided, pursued, and made happen without letting you know. Every choice will be different, because each choice they make will change them a little. What they have learned and carried with them will steer them in their next decision, and for the rest of their lives.

What can you do?

Prayers for Today

Pray for always having options and being given opportunities.

Pray for your son to take time with major decisions in order to weigh his options.

Pray that the choices your daughter makes will not close doors for future possibilities.

Pray for having all the information available during decisions, so no regrets come after them.

Pray for shared wisdom and guidance from people in your son's life as he uses others' advice in his choices.

Pray that the conflicting preferences of friends do not sway your daughter away from something she thinks is right for her.

Pray for satisfaction in decisions and personal growth from living through making life choices.

What else will you pray for?

36 Who Am I?

At some point during their first year, most college students fight a battle with their own identity. Everything your son has believed about his capability can be picked apart to its core. All the measures of accomplishment your daughter used in the past may have shifted their bases of reference and grading scales. They may even become completely irrelevant.

Success up till now has come from small accomplishments within a limited peer group for comparison. Your son probably grew up comparing himself to his classmates. His efforts ranked within a reasonable range and kept him competitive in anything he attempted. He managed to hit rockstar status on a few favorite activities. Your daughter may have progressed through classes with easy A's, had solos in school performances, won district and state championships in her sports, and held a student government office.

Then they went to college and became one of the many. Your son may be shocked to find that two other guys on his floor were also the captains of their soccer teams. Your daughter can audition for roles in ten different performances and never make the cast. They are not the superstars anymore. Their talents have not changed, but the talent pool has. Mr. Popularity may become Mr. Nobody when the fraternity he pledges turns him down. Your valedictorian daughter may struggle in her courses and find she needs tutoring help, even if she used to be the tutor for everybody else. Plenty of 4.0 GPA high school students can't handle their college level workloads. Another identity blow may come if your athlete student does not get chosen for their dream team, or has to take a second string alternate position after being a prized player in the past. They may not get the chances they planned on, and that may throw them off balance.

Labels in life can propel us, change us, and devastate us. If your daughter wraps too much of her identity around her previous labels, she may face some serious disappointments. She has very little chance of participating at the same super achievement level in all of her preferred activities. Too many other students are in the mix now. And, in reality, she should not keep doing the exact same things she did before. She needs a chance to learn and grow, too. Your son should look at his options and branch out into new interests. Your daughter should try new things which help her develop more of her character and abilities.

We like it when our students get some special designation. They have worked hard for years to make it to where they stand today. Their position in the pecking order made a difference in their opportunities and accolades. But that was then, this is now. Be ready for the unsteadiness that comes when their identity starts to crumble. Your star-athlete son who suffers a career-ending injury will struggle with his motivation and his grounding. If most of his life was intertwined with workouts, practices, and competitions for that sport, he will feel as if his world has collapsed around him. Your Student Council President daughter who spent weeks on a campaign will doubt her friendships and her connection on campus when the votes don't come her way in her next election. These things can blindside a previously confident student who planned the next few years based on that particular identity.

> Something for you to think about... some of us raised raincoat kids. When life throws its stormy nastiness at them, they suit up, face it all, and let it all slide off their raincoats. Some of our kids only carry umbrellas. They are not totally protected, but they are ready, so the stormy days they deal with don't make them too miserable. Others depend on the shelter-to-shelter approach,

making use of whatever they can find when showers start, but not letting the rain stop their progress. And some just get caught in unexpected downpours, feeling drenched and cursing the heavens for ruining their favorite shoes. The weatherman gets the forecast wrong sometimes, but he usually tells us of even the slightest chance of storms ahead. He's telling us to be on the lookout and stay prepared. So tell your student that. It's another Life Lesson. No one likes to get caught in the rain.   ---Monica Renahan

What can you do?

Prayers for Today

Pray that the changes and choices that come along give your daughter great options for her future.

Pray for your son's development of a personal identity above his labels or associations.

Pray for stability on the path, and for buffers from upsetting disruptions of dreams and plans.

Pray that your son tries new ways to participate as he pursues interests.

Pray for many opportunities to continue doing things they love while continuing to learn and grow.

Pray that your daughter sees rejection or lost opportunities as a place of new beginning, and enjoys the chance to find new interests.

What else will you pray for?

37 The Dangers of Living Life

We don't want to talk about it, but we need to face it. Almost every college newspaper has printed a campus tragedy issue at some point in its history. Some terrible event rocked the university and its community. News reporters from across the nation flocked to the school to cover every element of the story. Bad things happen, often to good people, and the world watches in the aftermath.

In just the past few months, headline stories of tragedies affecting college campuses have filled the news. The constant stream of information about terrible things happening to college students desensitizes us to the real nature of these events. Some tragedies repeat so often that you grow accustomed to hearing about them, like the stories of fraternity hazing and its fatal consequences. Other reports sound like badly written TV thrillers, with unbelievable events coming together in disastrous results. We hear of dorm fires, team bus crashes, sexual attacks, and random shootings happening on campuses. Coordinated disaster plans and emergency shelters exist because things can happen. Almost every university offers notification systems which can keep parents informed during a dangerous situation on campus. When those go off the first time, mom, you may experience a new feeling of concern you have probably never had before. Knowing that a serious safety issue currently exists on campus and not knowing if your daughter or son is nearby can cause major anxiety in even the calmest parent.

The news headlines covering major events make us uneasy about safety for our students. Then the stories get personal, as the individual identities of the humans involved come to light. Anyone watching can stop and say, "That could have been my daughter," or "He was just like my son." Stories that focus on one individual hit the hardest. Recent headlines told us a rideshare student made a deadly mistake getting in the wrong vehicle. Another news report gave us details of a student falling to her death while taking a selfie from high atop the campus bell tower. Every spring break ends with stories of students who never make it back to campus because of tragic accidents.

Now that your student lives on a college campus, you listen to these stories differently. Your perspective changes from unattached awareness to deep empathy for the people involved. Your Mom Instinct shifts into alert mode, wanting to learn every detail so you can reinforce prevention plans with your own student. This helps relieve the building tension and your fear that any harm will come to the one you love. These reactions are normal. We raise our sons and daughters to navigate the dangers of life and to protect themselves from harm. Our efforts stem from our wish that they live long lives while enjoying everything that life has to give. We do not want to accept even the slightest chance of them not growing old. We do not want to face what could become the worst experience of our lives. But that reality exists. That's why it hurts to hear these stories.

Thousands of people show up on college campuses every day and go home safely every night. Even if something bad happens on your campus, the tragedies you hear about will often involve people your son did not know. Your daughter may live in the same dorm as a student who was directly affected, but probably only recognizes her face as someone she had seen a few times before. If the tragedies hit closer to home, you may need to step up to help your son deal with the events. When he has a personal relationship with someone affected by a tragedy, like a connection through a team or a fraternity, he will need time to recover and need the support of his college community. He might need to step away and then may have difficulty returning to the campus.

Life may take a tragic turn as these events unfold, and you may find yourself dealing with your child's critical injury. Your world may stop spinning as you deal with unexpected news of how a terrible event on campus affected the one you love. Know that there are people willing to help you. Everyone from roommates all the way up to the University President may offer support and assistance. Even people dealing with their own grief and recovery within the tragedy will come alongside others who need help. Parents across the country who feel your pain will support you in prayer. In time, lessons will be learned, and sharing these experiences will help all of us move forward from these times of sorrow. It will not be easy. Lean on someone and take small steps to find your footing as you go. And know that I will keep praying for you, too.

What can you do?

Prayers for Today

Pray for all the moms who have experienced a tragedy, that their burdens will be lighter and they find peace.

Pray that your daughter avoids accidents and dangers on her campus.

Pray that your son avoids any reckless activities which could cause his own injuries after thoughtless decisions.

Pray that first responders can attend to your daughter's needs and restore safety in a dangerous situation.

Pray for your son's awareness of threats, so he avoids interacting with people who could put him in danger.

Pray for sustaining grace if a trauma occurs, for yourself and everyone else who needs it.

What else will you pray for?

38 Am I Speaking Japanese?

When parents say things, college students often appear to listen. They engage in the conversation and ask questions. Some will agree and then broaden the discussion to related topics. With all that confirmation of the communication going on, how do they get so confused about what we are trying to say?

Any time you begin a conversation you need to remind yourself of a few things: 1) your student's mind is juggling about twelve other things at this moment — five of which are more important to them than what you are saying; 2) they are making their own decisions now so your input is not the final word on the matter; and 3) your opinion may not even rank in the top five influences which will impact their decision.

If you have a distracted daughter who only catches pieces of conversations, you can get frustrated when you talk about something and all you hear back is "uh-huh." Listen closely… you might be able to hear tapping keys on her keyboard as she texts three other friends while you talk with her. You would expect a little more participation than that. You want to hear more from her than one-word responses like "great" and "fine." That is better than silence, you will admit, but it leaves a lot to be desired. If your son only agrees to your weekly update call because you insist on having it, he will not make the effort to share anything about his week.

It's natural for the dynamics of your relationship to change when your son goes off to college. You need to step back and let him take control of his life, and hope that he will make the effort to keep you involved in it. Your attempts to stay involved might fall on deaf ears, but keep trying. You can use a little creative outreach to keep the two-way street open for communication. In any conversation, the way you ask a question influences the way your listener responds. If your question enables a simple response, that's what you will get ("Did you like the movie?" will give you "Yeah.") Adjust your question so it needs more than one-word answers ("What was the movie like? What was your favorite part?").

If you maintained the family calendar and planned your daughter's activities in the past, you may feel she is missing out on things because she doesn't schedule her day the way you would. But she is in charge of that now. She will learn by her attempts and she will live with her mistakes. She may feel your system is not for her, even though she doesn't know yet if her new system works. Your ways were the old ways, and everything here is new. So, your input and advice may get lumped into that "old stuff is useless" pile when she moves on.

Another mom gave me a great tip: Find things to talk about which interest your son that don't involve giving him advice. Just have a conversation, as you would with a co-worker. You ask work associates about their weekends and listen to their stories without ever correcting them for choosing something you would not choose. You do not expect them to do what you would do.

Also, you need to realize that you may not be the expert for everything they need. If you can't hold back from offering advice, tell your daughter to seek some outside advice, too. That way you let her know that other people's expertise may matter more than yours on this. Maybe you are not the right person to help when your son talks about uploading his resume to a job search site because you are not even sure what that means. That's okay. The times have changed. What we did in the past worked for us, but that is not necessarily the best choice for today. Avoid advising about any areas you do not understand. That will reinforce your usefulness when you speak up and offer what you know. Then you can stay helpful in offering some relevant advice when it really counts.

If your communication with your son has hit shutdown mode, don't give up. Keep trying to include him in conversations instead of talking through his silence. If he gets distracted, tell him you understand if he's busy and you can talk to him later instead, and ask him when it would be good to call back.

If your communication has dwindled down to a few texts, don't flood his phone with daily reminders that you are thinking of him. A few are fine, but try to plan a time for an upcoming call and then leave him alone. Send him a reminder text a few hours before the call and give him a few things to think about that you want to discuss. Treat it like sending out an agenda before a meeting — you will give him a chance to get his mind ready for the conversation and let him know specific things you can accomplish by talking. It may seem like a drastic change from how you have interacted before. Just remember, everything else in your daughter's life changed when she started college, so changing this will work out, too.

What can you do?

Prayers for Today

Pray for patience as you establish new ways to communicate.

Pray that your conversations will be enough to fulfill you since you miss sharing your son's life.

Pray that you can ease into changes in your relationship and look for the positives for both you and your daughter.

Pray for awareness that you would appreciate more communication.

Pray that you will overcome the new challenges of having text and phone conversations instead of personal contact.

Pray for the time to share life with your son in meaningful discussions.

What else will you pray for?

39 Person of Interest

You watch from the sidelines, surprised and a little concerned. Your son changes more every time you see him. You have to step back as someone else steps into the role of Influencer in your daughter's life. It seems odd that your son willingly engages in debates over topics which garnered little more than shrugged shoulders and a "Whatever!" response in the past. You wonder what, or who, drew him into the conversation. Your once-reserved daughter changes her style, adding tattoos, piercings, and the goth look. Her wardrobe has become "anything, as long as it is black." As a mom, you can roll your eyes or cross your arms in disapproval, but that is it. What you say or think doesn't seem to matter. What you want your son to do and what he decides to do can be very different things. You wonder how his perspective could have changed so much in such a short time… it could be because of the Person of Interest.

The Person of Interest has an appeal. Maybe it's their carefree attitude toward living life when your daughter has grown up living by the expectations you set. It might involve seeing creative individuality after years of school uniforms and nondescript acceptable clothing. Maybe hearing personal opinions and passion about ideas has ignited something never sparked before. This new Person of Interest has taken over the influencing role which you held in the past. You lost that position when your daughter stepped into her new life on campus. Surrounded by thousands of unique individuals who did not look like her, think like her, or act like her, your daughter felt compelled to change something. Your son looked for a role model as he designed the New Me, or he combined a little of what he liked from a lot of different People of Interest. He wants to be interesting, too, so he adopts some appealing things from the people he finds interesting.

The funny thing is, your son may not have let someone have this much say in his life since he was seven. He always balked at your direction and found all kinds of things wrong with the life you provided instead of enjoying it. Now he may take this opportunity to absorb an influencer's appreciation of his hero-worshipping choices. The affirmation he gets from similar people will spur him on to try more expressions of his new persona. When new friends marvel at his new tattoo, he decides to add a few more. When the spiderweb jeans he wears catch the attention of strangers at the deli, he decides he will stop wearing plain ones anymore. The "Look at Me" need cries out, and it gets louder when people show they like what he does.

Take heart, mom. Watch a TV show from twenty years ago for a reminder that fads, fashions, and looks have come and gone throughout history. Personal choices change with every incoming class of freshmen. What seems important today will likely have no relevance next year. Most (but I admit, not all) of our students will settle into a more socially typical persona as they head off into the world after graduation. But, for the next four years, you may see things you just do not understand. Your daughter's focus on her Person of Interest will send her far off course from the path you think is better for her. Your son will take steps which you never thought he would consider as he follows his new muse.

Encourage the new expressions of your daughter's individuality which you like, and learn to tolerate the choices you don't. Things change, and the look or persona today may morph into something else next month. As your son moves closer to finding employment at graduation, more moderating influencers will take over. If the Career Counseling Office tells him his blue hair and tongue piercings will probably hold him back from getting a job in a major hospital, he will probably decide they need to go. It was fun while it lasted. He may feel that violates his personal rights of expression, but when the job offer he wants does not come, he probably will step down off that bandwagon.

Remember, it might take a lot to get it done, but even tattoos can be removed and body piercing holes can be filled by skilled surgeons. Nothing you do lasts forever anymore... except what gets shared on the internet!

What can you do?

Prayers for Today

Pray for your son's satisfaction with his identity and inner peace.

Pray that as your daughter makes choices, she considers the lasting effects they will have.

Pray for understanding that personal expression with reasonable limits can be just as effective as uninhibited personal expression.

Pray for your daughter to choose influencers based on worthy qualities instead of radical appeal.

Pray that your son will surround himself with friends who care about his opinions and engage him in new ideas.

Pray that your daughter feels her voice is being heard over the voice of her influencer.

What else will you pray for?

40 Sometimes It Helps to Admit Things Are Tough

As we build friendships with other moms, we grow as parents. Having friends around when the going gets tough can provide the support network that keeps you going. It may also keep you out of: a) jail; b) a mental hospital; or c) an early grave. Without opening up to others about my own doubts and concerns in my Mom World, I would not have heard about how different life can look in a normal family. Talking over coffee or chatting during power walks gave me a better understanding of other moms' challenges. Things that never came up in my world were daily struggles for some of my friends. Others had serious battles over things I easily brushed aside. Each of us had unique problems, but discussing all of them helped us work out some of our own related troubles.

I entered parenting thinking that other more experienced parents had clear and easy solutions for almost every problem. At least that is what the how-to-parent books and magazines convinced me! With the right advice or information, we could solve anything. Then I started living daily life as a parent. My needs were not addressed on the pages of the parenting books or in eight-minute morning talk show segments. My struggles seemed unique. They battled back every time I tried to manage them. I thought it was just me, since the things I needed didn't show up on the "Hot Topics for Parents" lists.

Then I started sharing my questions and struggles with other moms. I reached out for seasoned advice and for help in tying together the shreds of sanity in my crazy world. By talking and sharing, I found out that other moms were dealing with things, too. They just didn't talk about it much. We all had a public persona of calm and control, while we were tearing out our hair behind closed doors. If no one ever talked about failures and fears, then the rest of the group felt uncomfortable bringing up things like that. We held our "Things are great, thanks!" umbrellas high to keep the rainy world we lived in hidden. When one of us got real and let a little light in on the reality of her struggle, we would swarm around like worker bees, offering to help and supporting the weakened one. We all silently thanked heaven that it wasn't us or our kid. We didn't share that we were often facing something similarly daunting. Still, we secretly wished someone would come help us, too.

Fast-forward ten or fifteen years. Now you are chatting with friends at the grocery store. What is your conversation like? Do you revert to the 30-second highlight reel for each child and have a "Can-you-top-this?" moment? Or, do you ever try to give fair and balanced reporting, telling about a few successes and then mentioning a few challenges they have faced? When we open up the conversation to some weaknesses or struggles, we give our friends the opportunity to come alongside us and offer their support. Maybe they can offer some great advice or tell you about their own experience handling something similar. Maybe they will offer to pray for your child, and you, as you face this struggle. Maybe they have some great resource, information, or personal contact that could lead to resolving the whole thing! You will never know if you don't bring it up.

Stepping into honesty shoes can be uncomfortable. You might face mixed reactions. Some people will show a little pity. Some will brush off your needs since they are already dealing with enough of their own problems. But most friends will turn on their "ready to help" smile and stand by you in any way they can. Everyone's efforts will not be equal, and some well-intentioned advice and suggestions may complicate things more than they help. But in the end, our tribe rallies around us when the going gets tough and helps push us through our struggles.

What can you do?

Prayers for Today

Pray that you will become comfortable asking friends for advice or help when you need it.

Pray that you can resolve your concerns quickly.

Pray for your friends' openness and willingness to speak about their struggles when they could use your support.

Pray for your parenting skills, that you have developed what you need when you need it.

Pray that you encounter people who will be good counselors during troubling times.

Pray for wisdom in sorting through offers of help, focusing on the best resource available for resolving your difficulty.

What else will you pray for?

41   It Hurts When Another Mom Hurts

I asked a lot of moms for their input while I wrote the chapters of this book. Even though I learned a lot watching my two daughters go off to college, and their experiences could fill a book, I knew that our family's experiences uncovered only a tiny bit of all the things people face when they send their children off on their own for the first time. As I talked to more women, I heard some common stories, then listened to some unique challenges, and even had a few unsettling "Wait, what?... Really?" moments. Sending your student to college is never an easy process. This doesn't get easier after experiencing it with multiple children. Sure, some things become routine and your expectations get more focused after you have done it a few times. But each student is an individual, with her own expectations and dreams. Son #4 has his own needs and concerns which will come out at the first available opportunity, no matter what he heard and learned from his three older brothers about life at college.

Parents try, but they can't do it all, and no one handles it all perfectly. We do our best to prepare our kids and make sure they arrive at college ready to go. As the days and weeks go by, we see some areas which need a little attention and offer our help. We hear the stress in their voices and see their grades dropping, but we know the adjustment period has not ended yet. It's good to see them trying new things and finding new friends, even if their time management skills leave a lot to be desired. We make suggestions and try not to be too intrusive. We find a way to just let them grow up a little, even when it hurts to see them stumble.

We accommodate and empathize, as things get tough. Given the little we know about what's going on, we encourage the best we can. And that's all you can do sometimes. That's all you have to work with. If your son says things are okay every week when you talk to him, would you think otherwise? He seems to have it all together, even if he's learning through a few mistakes along the way. But, if you notice little signs that something isn't right, pay attention.

Be prepared, because right about then you might get knocked down by a shock wave. Sometimes things are a lot worse than you know. If he never tells you anything about the low points, he might be avoiding some overwhelming struggles he faces. Parents often find out only after a crisis moment happens. You may find that she has had meltdowns and panic episodes and rages against people in her life. You could hear that on one occasion, there were campus security officers involved. When life gets messy, some people (especially college students) hide things under their carpets and keep going. They find it too difficult to admit their failures to their expectation-filled parents. Handling troubles means hiding them or ignoring them completely. They move farther away in relationships while keeping the facade of the status quo. Some may turn to alcohol or drugs to ease their pains. Just like anyone struggling with a mental illness or an emotional disorder, they may need competent professional help to manage their feelings and thoughts. They usually will not seek out the help they need on their own.

No parent wants to get a call that her daughter has been taken to a hospital. No parent wants to see her son in danger. No friend wants to see her friend go through that with their children, either. News stories about tragedies on college campuses hit moms where we hurt. Not only do we fear for our own children, but we empathize with the moms of those students. Watching a friend facing troubles with her precious daughter will cause us to question the stability of the ground we stand on, too. We want the hurting to stop.

When things go wrong, many parents take on an unnecessary burden of responsibility and failure. "I should have seen this. I missed it," one says. "I didn't take control when I thought something wasn't right." Another remarks, "I didn't know that all this was going on." A mom shares, "I wish I had known about these people in her life." They witness the pain which their child is going through, and some blame themselves for not parenting well enough to prevent this from happening. That thinking causes more grief in a painful situation. They need to accept that the young adult in their presence has his own mind and has made his own choices, or that the illness which has overtaken him has overcome his thinking. It's not their fault as parents.

Campuses have many resources available to help students with mental and emotional struggles. Some students would never walk through their doors or use their helplines. Young adults can be invincible on the outside, and gasping for breath on the inside. Try to keep an eye out for signs of struggles. Start a conversation about overload and coming up for air. Find out what support services your student can access on campus. Tell her if you find free counseling services available for students, or if that would irritate her, tell her that you want to let her know in case she knows anyone who may need them. All kinds of people need them, but only some reach out for them. Sometimes it is good for them to hear they are not the only one who feels this way. They need to know they do not have to struggle alone. That should be today's Life Lesson for everyone, not just our college students.

What can you do?

Prayers for Today

Pray for other moms going through painful trials.

Pray that your son will not feel stretched beyond his capacity to handle his new challenges in college.

Pray that your daughter will take time to refresh and renew instead of hitting a breaking point.

Pray for upperclassmen who have managed these struggles before to set good examples for inexperienced students.

Pray for all campus staff to stay aware of any signs that students need assistance, and that people step in to help before anyone becomes overwhelmed.

Pray for accessible counseling resources when any students need them.

Pray for your son's patience and persistence in learning to deal with the challenges he faces.

What else will you pray for?

42 Giving Up for the Wrong Reason

Another mom told me this story: I know a sweet, dedicated, and compassionate international student. This girl will move mountains someday. She has loads of personality and potential. She came to this country to learn with one goal in mind: becoming a doctor. She has a clear vision. She doesn't want a Hollywood version of a medical practice, with shared patient loads, lunchtime golf breaks and glamorous office suites. She has no time for competitive Pre-med students who are more concerned with beating the MCAT test than learning the basics of care. She has more important goals. What pushes her and what she strives for are not generally understood by her classmates. She will never make a million dollars or drive a luxury car. She wants to return to her homeland and provide medical care for her people. Her family has taken on a great burden to send her to the U.S. for her education. They hope and pray she will succeed and come back to make them all stronger through her successes. Her future path is clear, and it leads back to her home.

It will… except if Biochemistry gets in the way.

Biochemistry has a reputation as one of those "Killer Classes" which stop college kids from pursuing their dreams. Also known as "Weed Out Classes," departments require these courses in degree programs. Almost every major has one or two; the lucky Pre-med students have more than a handful to complete. Most combine an overload of material, complicated math, obscure science, burdensome memorization, and hours of work expected outside the classroom. All for three credit hours. (Science doesn't have the corner on this market, though. Just ask a Business student about Statistics and Finance classes, or a Pre-law student about Contracts and Corporate Taxation.) This particular Weed Out Class has a well-deserved reputation. It is tough to understand, tough to memorize, and has pages and pages of difficult problems to work out which seem to have no connection to anything you have already learned.

This international student faced an overwhelming challenge in taking this course. She worked countless hours on her own and then spent more time with tutors. She attended every lecture and study session. She filled notebooks with attempts at problems and followed up with tutors for help when she could not go further. She watched friends and classmates drop out of the subject. Then she watched them also drop out of the Pre-med program, because they were failing this required course.

But she kept going. She told me, "I can't stop here. I'm halfway through this. I WANT to be a doctor. I don't need to be a Chemist to help my people. I'm not going to let these numbers and symbols on a page in my notebook keep me from doing that. What a waste my life would be if I did! I have a purpose and it's a whole lot bigger than this. I just need to get Biochemistry class behind me."

Maybe a lot of us would have different lives if someone had said that to us many years ago. Maybe your son or your daughter needs to hear that right now. They need to realize that one course should not stand in their way. It comes down to this: failing a required course means repeating that class. That is not the end of the world. That does not conclude your college story. Have your son find out if he can replace the course grade in his GPA if he retakes it. Some schools erase the first course completely and treat it like it never happened. Others show the first course and grade, but only use the replacement grade to calculate the GPA. Some students decide to repeat the class during a summer session when they only take one class. Not having the burden of other coursework at the same time and being able to focus on the tough subject usually improves performance. That means they get through it and move on.

Some schools have grade limits on required courses. Your son needs to find out if he is in a "B or Better," "Minimum of C," or "Just Pass the Class" situation. That will make a difference when considering whether to drop the class and retake it. Another thing to consider: if your daughter's career does not depend on being accepted for an advanced degree program, having a below-average grade for one course in her GPA/transcript really has no meaning if her overall GPA passes the requirements for graduation. Make sure they always check their own school's rules and the specific requirements for their major.

Retaking a course is not a failure. It's a sign that your son is willing to work hard to get what he wants. He will deepen his commitment by making the effort for the second time. Sometimes having a different teacher is all that they need. With other students, the coursework sinks in a little better the second time around. Still other people manage to ride out the easier first weeks with higher grades, having had the benefit of sitting through the entire course once already. Those early grades give them the buffer they need for their lower grades on harder exams later. It might sound like a game, but it might get them through it.

Now, take a little reality check here. Let's say your daughter wants to be an engineer. If she can't pass Calculus 101 after two tries, you need to have a discussion about all the harder math to come for that degree. In her case, it's not just a box to check on a requirements list. It's the foundation of all the tougher things on the horizon. Sadly, some dreams don't fit every person who wants them. Abilities matter in the long run.

Think about how many times in your life you have used a "do-over" card. If you're honest, probably hundreds. This might be the first big "do-over" your son needs to make. Be willing to support his effort as he tries to work things out. If your daughter thinks failing on the first attempt was the end of her dream, take the time to share with her how life is full of second chances and "do-overs," and we all are better for it.

What can you do?

Prayers for Today

Pray that your son works diligently to get through his tougher courses, even if he gets discouraged.

Pray for your daughter's professors as they prepare to teach and reach the students, for clear instruction covering all the necessary material.

Pray that they create exams which accurately measure the students' knowledge and capabilities.

Pray for your son to reach out to others for group help or tutoring when he reaches his limit of comprehension.

Pray for understanding and compassion when your daughter tells you she is struggling and may fail.

Pray for wise words to reassure your son, giving examples of your own "do-overs."

Pray for growth to come from each stage of learning.

What else will you pray for?

43 Some Do, Some Don't

Every college freshman starts off with high hopes and expectations about College Life. Some come prepared with life skills and maturity from their home experiences. Others are a little greener. Some parents drop their kids off with security blankets safely fastened around them to prevent any bumps and bruises along the way. They have raised their kids with guard rails around them and blinders on. These parents keep all the scary things away, and keep the bumpers in their bowling gutters so they couldn't fall in if they tried. Other parents drop-kick their kids out of the nest and hope for the best. "College is a learning experience, after all," they tell their wide-eyed child who is not quite ready for the world.

A little sweet freedom beckons some freshmen, and a bitter taste of impending doom calls to others. Your daughter may take a few steps on the edge of the nest and then joyfully jump off, straight into a graceful dive, and start gliding along on the easy breezes of a beautiful quad. Or, she might also take a peek over the edge of the nest, and then dig her claws into the branch and refuse to move, petrified at the thought of falling, or failing, or wildly flailing along while others watch her try.

There's a fairy tale about nature which most of us heard growing up. "When the momma bird knows her baby bird is ready to fly, she pushes him over to the edge of the nest, gives him a nudge out, and then, miraculously, he just starts flying!"

I know the truth. This does not happen every time. If a baby bird is not ready, he falls down and hurts himself when he hits the ground. While I was growing up, most summers my family fostered baby birds that left the nest too early and had painful crash landings on their first solo flights.

They may have tried to get out on their own without the right preparation and timing, too curious to see the world outside their nest. But most likely, their momma bird said, "He looks ready. All these other chicks are ready, so he has to be ready, too." And then the wild flailing starts… and then… Boom!

Some of our kids will soar. Some of them will sputter and flap and get their air at the last second while we hold our breath. Some of them will just hit with a face-first "Splat!" onto the quad. This is part of the growing process. We train them and prepare them for all the contingencies we can imagine. We fill their minds with character-building lessons, which set them up to face the world. But things are different now. If your daughter built her confidence depending on the support of friends, and now none of her friends have chosen the same school, she can feel defeated before she even starts. If your son has grown up knowing everyone in your community, and now faces a sea of strangers every day, he could fade into the sidelines with all the other unknowns unless he makes the effort to meet new people. You may not even know that he doesn't know how to approach a stranger and start a conversation since he never had to do it before!

Part of letting our kids go involves watching to see how they do: we probably don't know what training they missed. They won't know what they still need either, until it comes time to use it and it's not there. Then they will react in one of three ways: 1) they soar, 2) they fall and crash, or 3) they sputter along and get their wings and grow up a little along the way.

> This quote showed up on a friend's Facebook page: "All the popcorn kernels in a batch are prepared in the same pot, in the same heat, in the same oil, and yet, the kernels do not pop at the same time. Don't compare your child to other children. Their turn to pop is coming." - Author Unknown.

Maybe it will just take a little more oil and heat and time to get them popping. Even if they get a little burned on the edges, they're still a success.

A lot of us have scars from getting burned on the edges. Our battle wounds are a badge of honor. Military men show them proudly, saying, "I gave my all and have the scars to prove it." Every one of us has a few battle scars we could show off. We come through different challenges, winning different battles. We may have triumphed over things we do not talk about, making those private battle scars even more meaningful. As parents, we want to watch our kids take the first step out of the nest and soar, avoiding any battle scars. In reality, plenty of our kids will hit the ground when they drop. We hope their wounds will stay small, and stay as pain free as possible, but they will have a few battle scars for trying.

What can you do?

Prayers for Today

Pray for your son's willingness to face the new challenges in his future.

Pray that your daughter will not feel pressure to attempt things she is not ready to do, and pray for encouragement to keep working on her preparation for her moment to soar.

Pray that your son sees adventure, and not adversity, in the new world around him.

Pray that when your daughter takes off, she knows the challenges in her surroundings and the threats which might lie ahead.

Pray for patience as you encourage your unwilling son to take part in the new opportunities around him.

Pray for your daughter's willingness to share her failures and fears so you can give solid advice to help her on her way.

Pray for every student's maturity and development of life skills for their own benefit.

What else will you pray for?

Check-In Time

The topics in this book make you think about your student's college experience. What topics have surprised you? Which ones have moved to the top of your priority list? Did any encourage you to start a conversation with your student about something you had not considered before? Share your stories to let me know about your experiences at: **lifeasacollegemom101.wordpress.com** .

And keep praying!

44 Please Stay Out of The Headlines

A wise mom told me this story: After dropping off my daughter at her dorm one Sunday evening, I ran into another mom I knew in the parking lot. She had returned to her car and found something her son had left behind. After calling him, she waited for him to come back downstairs to get what he forgot. We were chatting when he arrived, so we stopped for a moment.

"Talking about me?" he asked with a big grin as he walked up.

"Of course not. With your boring life?" she replied with a wink my way. That made me laugh out loud. These two had a unique way of interacting. They made every sentence something to smile about. Their banter usually left me giggling, and it often gave me funny stories to share with my family and friends. It was never rude or crude. It usually included a good-natured jab or a flat-out insult, but never anything that really hurt the other person or embarrassed them. It was just their way. They would raise eyebrows and could deliver a little shock, but never cross the invisible line. People witnessing it for the first time might be a little surprised by it, but they never heard anything offensive.

As her son was leaving she reminded him, "Remember, you're here for one reason."

"Yes, I know. To make my Momma proud!" he shot back over his shoulder. He blew her a kiss and took a bow, as if taking applause for his performance.

"Okay. Sounds right," she called. As he went inside, she yelled at the top of her lungs, "STAY OUT OF THE HEADLINES!"

That took him by surprise. It also surprised about twenty other students as they walked near the front doors of the building. Everyone turned and looked our way. I was as shocked as they were, but I was looking toward him to see his reaction. Only then did I realize that my friend had ducked into her car after yelling, making it look like I was the crazy loud woman! Everyone else was staring at ME! She was sitting there just out of view, laughing uncontrollably. I had to take a moment and just laugh out loud again. She got me!

I could have felt embarrassed, irritated, or mortified by the situation. How could this "friend" set me up like that? But I laughed about it, because that's what they do. And getting upset and angry would have given me nothing except heartburn. It was a Life Lesson moment: Life's ups and downs are all a matter of how you take them. You can laugh them off or stay frustrated and offended. You can cry, or you can smile — it's all up to you.

I thought about looking at the online student news that week to make sure he had lived up to his end of the bargain and stayed out of the headlines. But I didn't. Instead, I made a point of telling that story to every person I could for weeks to come. I didn't mind being the one people were looking at. I didn't "doctor up" the details so I would look good in my version of what happened. I laid it all out and let people hear the whole thing, start to finish. And here's my reason why: I want more people to think about my story, and maybe even share my story, and listen to the message it tells. It's not the one about being embarrassed by a friend or having a witty rapport with a college kid. It's the message to STAY OUT OF THE HEADLINES. That's a Life Lesson if I ever heard one.

If this mom had yelled anything else, most of those students would have ignored her. They might have glanced her way, but they probably would have gone on without a second thought. "Stay out of the headlines" makes everyone stop, think, and look. It immediately brings up images of sordid stories and unimaginable crimes plastered across a page. Think back on your life for a moment. Have you stayed out of those headlines?

We all need to understand there are good headlines, too. We can fill our banner days with life-changing acts of service, encouragements, amazing discoveries, compassion, achievements, and building up others. We can make a difference to a few, or to more than we know. Headlines can proclaim great victories just as easily as great failures. You might walk away famous, or infamous, depending on what you do.

What will your headline read? And what are you encouraging your son to put in his? How will your daughter deal with a surprise headline that includes her name — will it be something she's proud of or a story she hides? We can all make some headlines right now; let's make them the right kind.

What can you do?

Prayers for Today

Pray that your son stays out of bad headlines and makes great headlines for himself throughout college.

Pray that your daughter can keep a good sense of humor whenever possible to deal with unexpected developments.

Pray that your son stays quick to forgive, quick to accept, and quick to encourage others.

Pray for a lighthearted mood to spread over the campus.

Pray for relief of stresses and concerns which prevent these students from enjoying life.

Pray for a shift in perspective from seeing life's irritations to seeing life's gifts.

What else will you pray for?

45 College ID

Every student at a college campus gets a College ID. This little card does great things: it gets your son into buildings, provides admission to campus functions, and proves who the person holding the card really is (if the picture matches the face). Your daughter might have the added benefit of access to campus cafeterias and her unused dining dollars with it. She may ride buses for free and get discounts at nearby stores by carrying it. But only if she has the ID. She needs to show it and it has to be currently activated. It proves she belongs and gets to use the benefits.

Why? Because your daughter is a student at that campus. She enrolled, she pays her tuition to be there, and she shows up. The label across her card reads "Student" — not Employee, Visitor, or Member. That declares her identity at that school. She may combine other roles into her campus experience, splitting her free time by jumping into her Athlete and Researcher and Part-Time Employee shoes. But, if those were the main reasons she was at that college, she wouldn't get a "Student" ID.

Some newcomers to college struggle with this. They find so many things to fill their days they forget the primary reason they are there. They uncover new passions and diversions, and would rather spend hours talking with new friends instead of going to classes and reading assignments alone in a library. Your son may feel time spent promoting an environmental issue is more important than reviewing vocabulary for a language course. Your daughter may complain that she wastes hours running accounting spreadsheets for her business courses when she could be making real money on her internet business. Those perspectives may be correct, but they miss the point of being there. Bring your son back to his College ID. Show him the word. It says "Student" for a reason.

They go to college to get an education. They need to fulfill requirements to get a degree. They may think that real life learning in a functioning business or an actual hospital is more important than learning concepts about how computers or chromosomes work. Hands-on learning helps, but the most important part of their education comes from learning how to learn. We forget that sometimes... and they forget it most of the time.

In the past, as graduation approached, some degree candidates had to complete internships or apprenticeships. They would willingly work under the direct supervision of an experienced professional who could show them how to function in their job. A few fields required it for certification, like nursing and teaching. Now, some students have a different perspective. They think they know everything important and don't like being told anything. They already know more than anybody else around them. A 22-year-old with a degree and an inflated confidence gene takes a job and shows up ready for everything. From day one, his ideas revolve around changing things to make it all work better for him. A recent graduate may feel completely comfortable telling her supervisor she doesn't think large staff meetings work unless everyone at any level can contribute during them. New hires expect promotions within months of taking a job, to keep moving up their career ladder. It does not matter that they have a lot to learn about what a job entails; they're bored and ready for something else.

More and more college degree programs have reinstated using semesters of "real work experience" as part of their graduation requirements to prepare students for their future roles. Colleges place students into work environments as student learners. From engineering to art history, and from broadcast media to political science, students get the chance to step into the real world but stay tethered to the learning process by assignments and activity requirements. They understand their role as observer-participants and know their upcoming graduation depends on successful completion and a positive evaluation at the end of the work experience. So, they are in a great position to learn something.

You might save your son a lot of time and effort if you start a conversation about work expectations with him. He may think he is ready, but he may not be ready for the real world. The world probably isn't ready for him yet, either. Talk about job and employee expectations with your daughter. Encourage her to look for opportunities to visit potential workplaces to watch her career in action. Shadowing someone in their field can be a life-changing experience. Be aware that it can go both ways, though: your son may get the proof he needs that it's right for him, but he may also see the real side of the job and decide it is not what he thought it would be. Also, the idea your daughter has about what a career offers can be quite different from what it's like to do that job eight or nine hours a day. Ask any nurse or teacher about that.

We learn throughout our lives, growing from what we experience as much as through our formal instruction. Spending time as a Student and learning how to learn has value for this portion of your son's life. Remind your daughter not to get ahead of the game. There is plenty of time for living in their future roles over the rest of their lives.

> A swimmer learns to swim by diving in. It's a good start, but unless he keeps going, he misses most of the experience. Learning is the same — it takes a big leap to jump into college knowledge, but the learning experience keeps going the rest of their lives.

What can you do?

Prayers for Today

Pray for acceptance of a learner's heart, with the right attitude and willingness to make the most of the experiences life gives.

Pray for your daughter's growth as she develops her career plan and considers who she wants to be.

Pray that your son's choices stay aligned with his strengths and goals, so he pursues the right mentors and learning opportunities.

Pray that they prioritize their studies as students and pick learning opportunities before other activities.

Pray for specific stages of the process throughout your daughter's college years, to keep progressing toward a goal.

Pray that your son will find a balance between observing and participating in his first career experiences.

Pray that your daughter uses her time as a student for exploration, character development, and determining her goals for the next stage of her life.

What else will you pray for?

46 It Won't Kill You

If you haven't had this talk with your son or daughter yet, do it soon. Pick up the phone and tell them you have something to say. It might not be relevant at the moment, but it's a Life Lesson they need to know:

> Sometimes life is harder than you want it to be.
> Sometimes you don't get your way.
> Sometimes things end up nothing like what you planned.
> But you keep going.

When I saw the explosion of comments on our college's parent page, I knew we had hit D-Day. I didn't even have to read them. The sheer quantity gave it away. It was Dorm Assignments Day. Suddenly there were 200 incensed parents who couldn't believe that their son or daughter didn't get any of their dorm preferences. Everybody can't have everything. With over 8,500 students to place on campus, I'm still in awe that the Housing Office manages to give anybody anything they actually want. They must use mathematical models and logarithms and special computer probability functions to power this process. It's all beyond me.

I remember the simple process they used years ago (I watched once). A dorm director assigned rooms to new students by pulling numbers out of a bowl. The number corresponded to a name on the alphabetical housing list. The director gave that person the first bed in the first available dorm room. Number two got the next open bed, and so on, till they filled all the rooms. Nobody had preferences. Nobody had options. You shared a room with the next person they chose. That was the way it was.

Fast forward 40 years. Now choices abound. For incoming freshmen who don't know the campus, selecting housing preferences is more complicated than selecting courses. Housing Offices have to create glossy brochures covering the special options that different dorm opportunities offer. It all boils down to this: if people are willing to pay extra for amenities, then the universities will offer them. Older dorms may cost a little less, but students in those miss out on single rooms with private baths or onsite food courts. Newer dorms with in-suite kitchens and fitness rooms offer an interesting upgrade from the basic dorms of years past. So, if you compared every dorm and you chose very carefully based on your personal preferences, of course you get upset if you don't get any of your top five choices. Sometimes life does that to you.

Let's get real. No matter what dorm your son lives in, he will meet people and do things on campus. No matter how much your daughter wanted the buildings with the in-room sinks and the loftable beds and the space to bring her futon, she will survive without them. Think about that before you complain. Compare the student feed to the parents' comments on the same day. Someone might post among their friends that they feel disappointed about their plans not working out, but other people will get on right away saying they will like so many things about the other dorm, or telling how great it was when they lived there. The students change their attitudes faster than the parents do. Sometimes your reactions stir up your son's ideas about what matters, and sometimes your son really doesn't care all that much. Your daughter just wants to get on campus and start college life.

Big dreams and plans for campus living sometimes need a little moderating by a wise parent before they blow out of proportion. We always want the best-case scenario. Life couldn't be better if all your son's plans worked out. But life can also be great in another arrangement, with some options he may not have considered. Praying to get all the perfect things may clarify the perfect plan in store for your daughter. It just might not be the plan you are expecting. We want the details to work out, but we really don't know what life will provide for them.

It won't kill them to miss out on getting their preferences or to learn to work around an obstacle which blocks their plans. Life will sometimes force your son to make accommodations when someone else's plans work out instead of what he wants. It actually will make him a little more ready for the world.

> Sometimes life is harder than you want it to be.
> Sometimes you don't get your way.
> Sometimes things end up nothing like what you planned.
> But you keep going.

What can you do?

Prayers for Today

Pray for understanding and flexibility when plans don't match outcomes.

Pray for your daughter to change her Missing Out mentality into a Try Different Things mentality.

Pray that your son learns to deal calmly with unplanned changes.

Pray for the administrators who deal with countless issues like these every day, that students and parents respect them and treat them kindly even in the face of disappointments.

Pray for the creation of bonded communities of students who flourish and develop lasting friendships.

Pray for the contentment of all students on campus.

What else will you pray for?

47   Being a Part of Things

For all the eager college students you find who want to get out and do things on campus, you can find just as many who would prefer watching from their dorm window as the world goes by. Some students spend the shortest time possible in their rooms each day, since there's a whole campus out there for them to enjoy. Others move as little as necessary from their home base and comfort zone, reluctantly facing the world outside only for class or to find food a few times a day. Each college student wants something different. Some may have day planners packed with meetings and activities. Yours may pencil in a few events a week to consider. He may also have only one date highlighted on his empty calendar: Last Day of Final Exams!

All students set their own pace for college life. Some overachieve, while others wonder what all the commotion is about. Many manage to complete a few resume-building activities along with their academics and sports. They may throw in some Social Justice events for the good of mankind, too. University calendars contain an overabundance of options, which even the best time management gurus couldn't manage to fit into their schedules. It all sits out there, available for people who are interested, who have the time, and who can squeeze them in and balance them with the rest of their schedules.

Students tackle the marathon of their college career day by day. Time passes slowly in some regards, and opportunities zip by in others. Sometimes they look in the rear window and see things they missed as they passed by. It can get depressing to find out about things they would have made time to do if they had known about them. They will also find times when there are so many things going on that they don't even want to get out of bed, since life has become a sprint from one event to the next. The key is finding a balance between being a part of everything and letting everything pass them by.

We know this from life experience, but our college kids probably have not lived it yet. They need to hear it. As your daughter chooses activities and tries to balance her involvement on campus with her schoolwork, she may need a little advice. She needs to hear that there's a difference between just showing up and truly engaging, and there are lots of different ways to be engaged. Think about a football game. Most of the fans are not engaging in the experience as much as the players on the field. The band members get very engaged during their halftime show, and then sit out the rest of the game in the stands. The announcer keeps his energy high from start to finish, no matter what happens in the stadium. Everybody has different roles to play, but they have all set their own limits on their engagement. Not everybody gives the same amount of effort. But they can all say, "I was at the game."

Sometimes the roles switch for these same groups as they go to the next activity. If you play in the band and have a two-hour concert later that night, you prepare to give a lot more effort than the amount you put into the football game experience. If you transition from game announcer to concert announcer, you might only talk for a total of four minutes over the whole night. Still, they both can say, "I was at the concert."

Some enthusiastic college kids take on lots of roles in their activities and give every one of them all they've got. They have not found the right way to balance all the things they want to do. They will learn to take the lead in a few things, and to let other people take control of the rest. Sometimes, playing a small, supporting role can turn out more rewarding than managing all the details. It's easier to strike up friendships working right alongside someone than when you're overseeing everything happening at an event. If you focus on all the details, you miss the human interaction going on. Encourage your son to open up to new opportunities and do new things, but remind him he doesn't have to be in charge of everything he does. Be ready to offer a bit of advice when it sounds as if your daughter has too many things on her plate to manage. They need to make their own decisions and learn in their attempts, but they can also use your wisdom and concern to figure things out before they hit the overload point.

What can you do?

Prayers for Today

Pray for opportunities to grow as a leader and to grow as a participant.

Pray for your daughter to balance time commitments and efforts as she chooses her activities.

Pray that your son finds good role models in advisors and upperclassmen who will influence him in successfully creating an enjoyable college experience.

Pray for the minimizing of rear-window regrets, wishing for lost opportunities and wanting what other people chose.

Pray that your daughter reaches out to others as she starts new adventures, to share those experiences with friends.

Pray for your son's awareness when things are once-in-a-lifetime opportunities, so he makes the effort to participate in them when he has the chance.

What else will you pray for?

48 Please Stop the OMGs

Another mom told me this story: When my daughter and I were at a welcome week seminar, we met a very nice international student and his mom. They originally planned to attend an International Student Orientation a few weeks earlier, but travel delays and cancelled flights had made them miss it. This was their first real exposure to the campus and to the US; the college had handled their entire international admissions process through Skype interviews and contact with an advisor who held meetings for interested students in their home country.

During the seminar, the counselors directed parents to do a few things if they had time that day, to save their student some time waiting in lines the next morning. The list included things like "Stop and drop off your immunization records if you have them," or "Set up your password access for your billing and verify your mailing address is correct." A few times the international student's mom turned to us and whispered a quick question about what we needed to complete. I helped her with directions to a building and by showing her a form to use from our packets. She was trying to take detailed notes on everything.

One speaker mentioned, "Parents, one of the best things you can do is handle the Parking Pass. Those lines are always long because everyone wants one, and it's absolutely necessary to have one before tomorrow afternoon, because that's when our patrols start ticketing."

She turned back to us and whispered, "Ticketing??"

Another mom answered, trying to simplify, "Yes, for violating the rule by not having the parking pass, they write you a ticket and then you have to pay a fine. It's something like $40, I heard, and they're ruthless!"

"And you have to have it with you all the time, starting tomorrow?" the woman asked, still not sure she understood.

We all nodded, so she smiled and she started writing something in her notes as the next speaker started her segment.

Later that evening, I ran into this mom and her son. We each talked about things we accomplished (like finding the financial aid office and not getting lost), as proud as blue-ribbon winners. Then she said, "And I made sure my son would not get a ticket tomorrow. Here is his Parking Pass." She pulled out a sticker and a receipt.

"What do you have that for?" her son asked, very confused.

"They told us to handle it today for you. I don't want you to get fines. And he was right, there was an hour wait."

He put his hand over his eyes. "OMG! OMG!" was all he could say. A very heated conversation followed in a language I didn't understand. Thankfully, it was short. And it turned back to English at the end.

"I can't even drive in our own country! I don't have a license. I can't use this! I can't believe you bought this!" he told her.

Then it all made sense to me. She had followed instructions and handled something like she was told. What she didn't realize was that what they were saying didn't apply to her.

166

I've been there. And I felt her pain. Her son was acting as if she had humiliated him, again, and she was a burden rather than a help at this point. He also felt frustrated that she wasted $195 on something worthless to him. Instead of letting him wallow any deeper in his personal mud puddle, I startled him back to reality by speaking up.

"Oh, that's easy to handle," I said. "I can take you back over there right now and get this refunded. Remember, they told us that the office stays open until 8 pm. Let's catch that shuttle right there before it leaves." I motioned toward the bus stop so she would see that it was almost finished loading.

His mother was still reeling from her failure and her son's rebuke, but she looked at me with grateful eyes and nodded. "Thank you so much for helping me," she said quietly.

We've all been in a bad situation before. It's a pretty miserable feeling. It's a feeling we all should try to remember before we start criticizing someone else. It happens online all the time. I have seen the degrading OMG replies time after time. When someone posts a simple question on a college parent site, some mom trying to be helpful writes a reply about something she has done. That sets the battleground. It's that simple. A few replies may be supportive, and then you read the one that drops an atom bomb.

"OMG! I can't believe you would do that. She's at college now. She's an adult. What's next, are you going to show up and change her sheets and do her laundry? Does her mommy still have to arrange everything in her life? Let her do it!!!!!!!!!"

I guess the only response to reading that is, "OMG! I can't believe YOU just said THAT!"

167

Each of us approaches parenting a little differently, and each of our kids has learned different life skills. Things my daughter handled capably on her own at age nine were never even tried by her new roommate. I chose to do some things for my kids so they would spend more time on their activities and their advanced curriculum workloads, but that meant they were not old pros at housework or cooking when they showed up on campus. But they were pretty savvy with their money, while some friends spent tons on convenience store overcharges and impulse purchases. All college students have areas they excel in, and other things they are totally clueless about… and the same goes for every other human being on the planet. Here's what it boils down to: my kid is not better than your kid and yours isn't better than mine; you're not the best parent in the world and I'm not either; and we all could use a hand to help us, not slap us, once in a while.

If you're not in a robe and sitting on a bench, please stop judging! Make the world a little easier to get along in.

PS — And if you want to tell me something (critiques or praises) about what I said here, feel free to say whatever you would like on my blog: **www.lifeasacollegemom101.wordpress.com**.

I'll admit, I have learned plenty from things people have shared. That's what this book is all about.

What can you do?

Prayers for Today

Pray that you avoid missteps and stay on the right path as you handle responsibilities.

Pray that your son is prepared to face the challenges of daily life on campus.

Pray that you can be helpful to other moms by sharing your knowledge and experiences.

Pray that those who are looking for answers will find your suggestions, and that they can use and appreciate the information.

Pray that your daughter will share her skills with her friends who need assistance.

Pray that your son's friends will have patience with him when he lacks skills, and willingly offer to help him.

Pray that your daughter always feels comfortable asking you for advice, but that you step back as she tries to master things on her own.

What else will you pray for?

49 From This Day Forward

A lot of things change for moms when college students move away to start a new year. Life at home won't be the same. One face will not appear at the dinner table and a bed will go empty. One chunk of your time commitments will clear away now. Those are the obvious changes.

Many moms find that the relationships among the family members will also change. When your oldest leaves, the rest of the family can face a wide range of impacts on everyday life. Duties and responsibilities can shift to younger siblings, who may not be ready for those roles. If the oldest took charge when Mom and Dad left, you need to train someone new now. They may not be willing to step up. You probably spent hours going over rules and duties and warnings and emergency plans with your oldest to prepare him for your absence. You did not involve your younger children, or they were too little to understand when all the teaching was going on. Now you need them to take a responsible role, but you never gave them the training to take command. Don't count on a seamless transition of authority here.

Daily obligations outside the home may fall on your other children now, too. You may want your son to take on the Shuttle Bus Driver responsibilities for other family members, to fill the gap left by his college-bound sister. That younger sibling may have different ideas about wanting to drive. If the older one always had the car, her younger brother may not have had time to develop his skills and competence. He may not even want to drive, since someone always took him where he needed to go. Now that you need him in the transportation equation, you realize he's not ready for the job.

Family dynamics change as each child grows and moves on, but never more than when your youngest leaves the house. You need to be ready for some unexpected life adjustments and unplanned emotions. Some moms hit empty nesting with celebrations; others feel a great loss as their connections with the world dwindle away. Plenty of the things that fill our days as moms revolve around our kids' lives. You could face a rocky transition as those connections fade away.

Think about the amount of time you spent with other parents at high school activities and other school events over the past four years. Now wipe the slate clean. You may not spend any time on campus all semester. If you are lucky, your college may have one Parent's Weekend in the fall where you can interact with other moms. If you show up for football games or soccer matches, you may run into a few more. No more working for hours on fundraisers or sitting with other parents in the visitor stands at all the away games. Your chances to do anything with any parents except your closest friends might evaporate completely. The calendar will be the emptiest it has been for the past 12 years. This takes some getting used to; and it takes a shift in perspective, too. You have plenty ahead of you.

It might take some effort, but it's worth it to rekindle old friendships and try to get together with other moms after your kids go away to college. It will help to hear about how their kids are tackling the newness of college and find out your worries and questions are just like everyone else's. You all care about your kids and want the best for them, even if you might not agree on what that is. Sometimes hearing stories of how things are going for others helps prepare you for things just over the horizon in your daughter's experiences. Listening to different perspectives on which things worked, and which ones did not, gives you hope when it seems nothing is going right for your son. And getting a few stories to tell your daughter about her old friends may remind her that other people are going through what she's going through, too. It's good to stay connected, even if it's not very often, as long as it brings you a smile to do it.

Finally, but probably most important to remember and address, your spouse or partner will be in the middle of all this, too. If he's a no-emotions-kind-of-a-guy, he may handle it on the outside like it's no big deal. He feels the changes. He sees the vacant chairs. He realizes his gardening buddy isn't around anymore. Even if he doesn't want to acknowledge it, it has made an impact on him. And he probably notices that you are not quite yourself, too.

The gaps left when they go away are hard to fill and harder to explain. If you get a chance to talk to younger kids about missing their brother with your spouse present, it might help him realize everybody else feels it, too. Then try to bring it up when you can talk alone, away from other family members. Give him the chance to talk, but don't push. Maybe simply knowing somebody knows will settle his mind. Everyone is different! (Truly an understatement!) Making the effort may help you come together to support each other as you navigate through this new stage of your lives. Give it time. As your parenting identity fades and becomes less important in your relationship, it opens up new spaces to start something new between you.

I have to close this chapter with this story a mom shared with me:

> I lived through it, so now I have a new perspective on how our family could change when my son left for college. Sure, everybody was missing him in their own way. His younger brothers missed the rides he would give them to their baseball practices and having battles against him on the Xbox. His dad missed shooting a few rounds of hoops with him, talking about his plans and his college options and the hopes he had for his future. I missed having someone who enjoyed the adventure of trying a

new meal I had seen on some cooking podcast, with new spices or combinations of foods I never would have thought to use. He would take a bite, smile and say, "Now, this is interesting... but this is what I think you should do next time..." and we would laugh and enjoy the rest of the less-than-perfect creation together.

There was a definite void, but we were each managing on our own, never bringing it up. Then our dog Pilot decided that someone he cared about was missing and no one else was doing anything about it. He started taking things we needed and dropping them on my son's empty bed, like a cell phone and then my purse and even my younger son's soccer cleats. The dog knew that we would go looking for them, and he figured we would realize that my son was missing when we found them in his empty room. I guess he thought we needed the reminder that he was gone. How far from the truth that was!

After the fourth hunt for a missing item led me to his room, it all made sense to me. It really hit me that someone else realized he was gone, too. The effect was beyond just me and my world. I sat down on the bed and cried, while my dog stayed next to me with his chin on my knee, sharing my sorrow. Without saying a word, Pilot wound up being the best counselor I could have asked for. Later I told the story to my husband, and then to my sons. It gave us a way to share that we were all missing him, and it was okay to feel that way. We had buried our emotions and moved on with life, and it took our dog to dig them up for us again.

What can you do?

Prayers for today

Pray for parenting transitions and family changes to come smoothly, with as little trouble as possible.

Pray that your son realizes that the ones he loves are missing him, but they want him to enjoy his college adventure.

Pray that each family member resolves their feelings of missing your college student.

Pray for reasonable expectations as younger siblings take on new roles.

Pray that the relationship you have with your spouse deepens as your family dynamics change.

Pray that the moments of sadness are balanced with moments of joy as your daughter emerges into adulthood.

Pray for an awareness of the needs of all of your loved ones (and your own needs, too), as you share more time together.

Pray for your friends as they experience these transitions in their own families, too.

Pray for open dialogues among friends that offer support and advice in dealing with the new challenges you are all facing.

What else will you pray for?

50 Just Ask

No matter how many topics I cover, something new always comes along to pray about. Life changes daily on a college campus. A new priority shuffles to the top of your son's planner every day: cramming for midterms overtakes his life one day, and then his focus completely shifts to practicing with his undefeated soccer team the next. You may not know any of the particulars of your daughter's busy schedule. You listen for details while you talk and get snippets that she's worried about her lab practical and finishing her application for an internship. She also mentions the fact that her computer screen has dark bands on it but she can't give it up for four days to get it fixed, and she doesn't want to lose everything on it if it crashes. You can't begin to know what to pray about. Unless you ask.

> A very wise college mom shared with me: I looked forward to any time I could catch up with my son on the phone. It filled in a lot of the details that texting leaves out. We chatted about friends and classes. We discussed plans and opportunities to do new things. We usually spent longer than we imagined, and then wrapped up conversations quickly as one of us rushed off to do something else. Too often I realized after hanging up that I missed sharing some important items and needed to speak again soon. Thinking about that, I began to wonder if there were things he wanted to talk about, but didn't. Maybe he had some things on his mind that he wished he had shared with me, too.
>
> I started making sure I asked a special question before we ended our calls: "Is there anything you want me to pray about for you?" The first few times, because it was an unusual question, I didn't hear any deep or moving requests. It took a little getting used to. I

brought up topics like the ones I used already in my prayers for him. After a while, I heard a few more meaningful replies. Once, my son even asked for something regarding his future plans that I had prayed about for him on my own the night before. We shared an amazing time of connection as he felt deeply supported and encouraged by prayers sent out on his behalf even before he could tell me about his worries.

Until I started asking, I prayed for his preparation more than any specific needs. They are both wonderful expressions of faith, but they have different significances. Praying through the specific things they need will connect you to what they are going through right now, in addition to praying for their preparation to handle the things yet to come.

That question will make some of them feel uncomfortable. The level of communication you have with your son will limit how much he shares with you. Your daughter's hesitation to speak about her own worries or shortcomings may stop her from sharing her most pressing needs. Just ask. Then ask again another time. Make it a habit and soon it can set the foundation of a new conversation platform. If you already tried this and did not get a great response, try another option: "Who else around you needs some prayers right now?" By shifting the focus off of them, they might open up about the things going on around them which are influencing them. That will give you a better picture of the struggles in their world. If neither way works, just stay tuned in for glimpses of the important things while you talk, and offer your prayers up anyway. God already knows the details.

Someday, at the end of a time of sharing, you might even hear, "Is there anything I can pray about for you, Mom?"

What can you do?

Prayers for Today

Pray for opportunities to listen to your daughter's prayer needs

Pray that the level of sharing between you deepens.

Pray that your son becomes comfortable discussing his concerns.

Pray that your daughter's challenges resolve quickly with little disruption or difficulty.

Pray for your heightened awareness of asking your son about his specific prayer requests.

Pray for dedicated time and effort in supporting your daughter in prayer.

Pray in gratitude for answered prayers and continued blessings.

What else will you pray for?

The Last Chapter

As we walked through this book together, we prayed for a wide range of things. We approached a new chapter of life and its new challenges with a steadfast resolve to pray through it. Now we have blanketed our daughters and sons with unending support through our specific and relevant prayers. We have found new hope in the provision of God.

The journey has opened our eyes to new concerns. It has taken us into unfamiliar territory and through unwanted bends in the road. We focused our prayers on what we thought they needed, but also on what we ourselves needed. Friends have shared their wisdom and support as they told us their experiences. Strangers have shared their stories, teaching us lessons and giving us new perspectives. Campus Leaders have shared new areas of concern which they see develop daily. Every element deserves our attention and time in prayer.

You may have thought a few chapters discussed things that didn't apply to your student. Be thankful! Instead of skipping the topic entirely, try going back now. Take another look at the chapter and pray that your son will remain free of these concerns. Also pray that your daughter can be the support and encouragement for others as they struggle with this part of college life. Pray that as their lives change over their four years on campus they will be prepared to deal with these needs when they arise.

Now, I encourage you to turn back to Chapter One and start again. Every day brings a new challenge, and our daughters and sons need our prayerful support. Freely move throughout the topics as you need them. Some days you might stop after reading just one with a lot to ponder. On calmer days, keep progressing through the chapters. Even though you have read them before, they may have a completely different relevance the next time because of the current situation you have in front of you.

I also encourage you to think about a friend who could use the wisdom in this book. Pray for her as she faces her own struggles in sending her student to college. Maybe it's time to send her a copy with an encouraging note attached. Think about how pleased you would feel if someone sent you a kind gift out of the blue to help you get through your day. Share this book with someone who could use it. Another way you could help moms find out about it is by mentioning you read it on your College Parents site (or one for your high school's parent group). Sharing how it was a helpful resource to you will make it even more useful to more moms. You found it and used it; now help another mom find it and use it, too.

Extra copies of this book can be purchased in bulk for group fundraising or educational use. Learn about the program details online at: **www.lifeasacollegemom101.wordpress.com**.

You can also spread some generosity and sponsor a copy of this book for another mom with our **Share the Story** program. Help cover the costs of producing the books we give away to moms of first generation college students. You can sponsor one copy or as many as you can provide. Please see the details at: **www.lifeasacollegemom101.wordpress.com**. Thanks for helping, and thanks for reading!

Before you go, please join my blog and say hello on my website so I can keep sending more encouragement during your college parenting experience! Go to: **www.lifeasacollegemom101.wordpress.com**

We started our journey together with this verse from the Bible, and we'll end with it here: Philippians 4:6-7 (NIV) tells us: "Do not be anxious in anything, but in everything, by prayer and petition, with thanksgiving, present your requests to God. And the peace of God, which transcends all understanding, will guard your hearts and minds in Christ Jesus."

Topic Index by Chapter

Topic Index by Chapter

Topic Index by Chapter

Made in United States
North Haven, CT
11 August 2022

22619928R00104